CULTURE AND IDENTITY

Borgo Press Books by FRANCIS JARMAN

Culture and Identity (editor)
Encountering the Other (editor)
The Gate of Lemnos: A Science Fiction Novel
Girls Will Be Girls: A Play
Intercultural Communication in Action (editor)
Invictus: A Play
Lip Service: A Play
A Star Fell: A Play
*White Skin, Dark Skin, Power, Dream: Collected Essays on
    Literature & Culture*

CULTURE AND IDENTITY

FRANCIS JARMAN, EDITOR

THE BORGO PRESS
MMXII

Borgo Perspectives on Intercultural Communication
Number Three

CULTURE AND IDENTITY

FIRST EDITION

Published by Wildside Press LLC

www.wildsidebooks.com

DEDICATION

For LAKSHMAN V. K. SOJITRA

CONTENTS

INTRODUCTION
CULTURAL IDENTITY

INTEGRATION AND ASSIMILATION are not the same thing. Three hundred years ago French Protestants (the "Huguenots"), fleeing from religious persecution or looking for better economic opportunities (or both), came to settle in Germany. Over generations they became so much part of the host society that now there is seldom much left of their original culture, other than their French-sounding names. Something very similar seems to have happened in many of the families of people from Poland or Czechoslovakia who came to Britain during the Second World War. I myself came to live and work in Germany more than thirty years ago, and I am (I hope) well integrated into German society—but I have not been assimilated. Not infrequently I'll come into conflict with German friends or colleagues, or there'll be a bad misunderstanding. Reflecting afterwards on the possible cause, I'll find myself ruefully concluding, "Oh dear, I put my foot in it again". It may have been out of tactlessness or from insensitivity, but most often it will have been because of a (to me) harmless moment of flippancy, irony or humor. Now these are reasonably acceptable characteristics of everyday British behaviour, but they are not things that Germans are always comfortable with. Of course, after all those years in Germany, I should have known better—but, like it or not, once in a while my British socialization will out. *You can take the boy out of Britain, but you can't take Britain out of the boy...*

My children, in contrast, who were born and raised in

Germany, *are* assimilated, and their being able to speak English better than most of their German contemporaries doesn't substantially change that.

However, the differences between ethnic groups within a society, especially those between the host culture and the cultures of immigrant minorities, tend to be more deep-seated than those that normally exist between the British and the Germans, or between the Germans and the French—*i.e.*, the situation is not so much one of *multiculturalism* as one of *multivaluism*. The challenge is then to find a degree of integration that will nevertheless enable harmonious social relations. This will entail compromises having to be made on both sides (and it will be the members of incoming groups who will be obliged to make the principal concessions, a point that *bien-pensant* multiculturalists have found extraordinarily difficult to understand). Whatever solution is reached will need to allow for the retention of identity-giving cultural features and religious beliefs, keeping the charm of "exotic" cultural difference alive and providing suitable conditions for constructive but also synergistic cooperation. Taking Britain (and population groups originally from the Indian Subcontinent) as an example: whereas the Sikhs have generally achieved this level of integration, many of Britain's Muslims noticeably haven't.

Such a solution requires from minority groups a substantial cultural make-over, and from everyone concerned a wearisome process of cultural fine-tuning and finessing. This is by no means easy! Various countries in modern times have gone down the road of multi-ethnicity. It may still be too early to judge the success of such varying experiments as Brazil, Singapore, Malaysia, *etc.*, or even of Belgium. Yugoslavia failed spectacularly. A fascinating undertaking that has just got underway is the project to forge a "rainbow nation" in South Africa. And perhaps (a very big perhaps) a course like this could lead to a long-term two-nation solution to the dilemma of what used to be called the Holy Land, provided that Israeli

Jews and Palestinians remain in the majority in their respective countries—unfortunately, religious extremists, political opportunists and meddlesome neighbors are likely to prevent this from happening. Broadly speaking, the problems tend to be massive and the solutions frequently complex (and quite unlike the respective answers offered by bigoted cultural purists and by naïve multiculturalists).

Since 9/11, and the subsequent terror attacks in Bali, Madrid, London and elsewhere, "strong" multiculturalism has become increasingly unfashionable, and many advocates of diversity have turned to *transnationalist* and *transculturalist* approaches. These view culture as a transaction, a fleeting construct; they rightly reject essentialism and ethnocentrism to the extent to which these reduce culture to the monolithic, hegemonic code of a nation-state. Transcultural identity is created in the interstices between cultures and in the interaction between different cultural groups. It is postmodern, even deconstructive, yet at the same time a "turbo-version" of that hoary old model, the Melting Pot, though presumably leading to a different end result.

It may well be that we are what we choose to be (there is an echo of existentialism here), but that should not mean an outright dismissal of the idea of cultural identity, merely that our essentialism must be contingent, diachronic and based on critical self-awareness. [The final contribution to this volume returns to this subject.]

Spectacular advances in communications and cheap travel in recent years have certainly created an appropriate enabling framework for transculturalism, to the point of giving members of immigrant communities who are socially, educationally and linguistically insecure—Mexican-Americans in the United States are sometimes given as an example—an excuse for *not* trying to learn the language of the host community and for *not* making strenuous efforts to integrate (whereas those who are more robust and ambitious will want to take this route, out of a desire to succeed and with the aim of maximizing their social and cultural opportunities).

It is without doubt an appealing theory for such rejectionists; for sophisticated transients, those who are intellectually and culturally self-confident, but who chafe at the petty restrictions—and the responsibilities—imposed on them by social conventions; and for self-indulgent itinerants, both those who do transience for real (such as the international jet set) and those who merely flirt with it (the middle-class hippies, the rock-and-roll gypsies and "free spirits"). Most transients, though, lack the resources, material and educational, to enjoy their condition, which is a stressful and demanding one, and they cling to some at least of their cultural roots. For them, rootlessness is not "sexy"—it doesn't mean freedom, it means anomie, risk, conflict, frustration and even despair.

THIS IS THE third book in a series with the broader title *Borgo Perspectives on Intercultural Communication*. The essays in this volume include both **autobiographical accounts** and **specialized academic case studies**. Most of the contributors are colleagues, former colleagues, former students or friends of mine (these are overlapping categories), many from the University of Hildesheim in Germany, but there are also contributions from further afield. The authors come from Britain, Egypt, Germany, India, Ireland and Mexico.

The first essay outlines a number of different concepts of identity, using the troubled island of Cyprus as an example (NIEDERWIPPER); then comes a study of a remarkable feature of the Italian self-image, namely *bella figura* (BRÜNIG), and an investigation of auto- and heterostereotypes of the Czechs, especially where these involve their awkward neighbors, the Germans (KRESS); next, autobiographical accounts of the difficulties of cultural adjustment between the two Germanies, East and West (WERNER), and between Mexico and Germany (CAMACHO-MOHR), and an interview with a colorful and outspoken intercultural commentator (GERAGHTY); then, a series of literature-oriented essays focusing on the quandary of Japanese-Americans in the Second World War (TAWHID AHMED), on the

Indian poet Ranjit Hoskoté, who has made cultural identity one of his central themes (TELGE), on drama (and its translation) in the "stateless nations" of Scotland and Quebec (AUGUSTIN), on two playwrights from very different cultures but with similar concerns (ABDEL HAFEEZ), and on the work of a research center for Indian literature in English and in translation (PAUL); there follows a survey of the varying responses to love in different cultures (EINHOFF); and, finally, a discussion of cultural identity as both an obstacle and an opportunity (JARMAN).

The listings of "References" at the end of some of the contributions are precisely that—listings of works directly referred to or quoted from—and are not intended to be full academic bibliographies. Where online sources are given, the date of most recent access is uniformly January 20th, 2012.

The views expressed in these essays are not necessarily those of the editor, the publisher or of fellow contributors.

THE FIRST VOLUME in the series, *Encountering the Other*, offered a selection of widely differing personal descriptions of encounters with cultural Otherness; and essays about intercultural aspects of politeness, everyday contact, seduction, and war; the second, *Intercultural Communication in Action*, was about the practical side of intercultural communication, in particular the internet, the media and journalism, education, and language.

The series has two "homes". The first is the Institute of Intercultural Communication at Hildesheim University, Germany, which is where I happen to teach and research. The second is Wildside's Borgo Press, where I should like to thank my editor, Professor Michael Burgess, for his encouragement, support and unfailing patience.

—FRANCIS JARMAN
Hildesheim, Germany
January 2012

ANATOMIZING CONCEPTS OF IDENTITY

THE EXAMPLE OF CYPRUS

BY TAINA NIEDERWIPPER

THE CONCEPT OF IDENTITY can truly be regarded an "export hit" of modernity (see Baumeister 1986). Originating in the field of philosophical logic, it made its way into the discipline of psychology (Bausinger 1982, 12) and from there, figuratively, it conquered the world. Today, identity is everywhere. But what exactly *is* identity, and what are the challenges and constraints that it faces?

Identity is comprised of characteristics we believe to be essential for describing ourselves, which range from personal attributes to groups we feel like belonging to. While the concept of *personal identity* refers to our individualistic and very own feelings of being and belonging (Bausinger, 15), *collective identities* are concerned with affiliations to groups constituted by social bonds, which grow out of shared perceptions and beliefs and evoke feelings of solidarity within and loyalties to the group (Fligstein 2008, 127). From a constructivist point of view, identities are mental, social constructs, being neither given nor natural (Fearon / Wendt 2002, 57), which come into being through social interactions (Ulbert 2006, 409). These interactions are not limited to concrete *visible* activities, but also include *mental* ones such as perception. Accordingly, Eickelpasch / Rademacher (2004, 14) have described identities as "construction sites"; they are projects in progress. This perspective allows us to treat identity as a flexible, dynamic and adaptable concept, something that is not at all static or narrowing. Yet despite its dynamic character, identity can nevertheless provide an important framework of orientation.

The fact that identities are pluralistic and that people do have multiple collective identities (Fligstein, 128) raises the question as to whether, and if so how, different collective identities can coexist. To answer this, it seems reasonable to imagine culture, as Geert Hofstede does (1991, 6), as coming in layers which constitute different concepts of identity. These layers, arranged like those of an onion, differ in their level of visibility to outsiders. This means that while symbols of different identities are visible and detectable from outside, underlying values remain invisible and therefore harder to detect and understand for someone not sharing in that same culture. But different identity layers, being adopted by the same person, do not necessarily have to be in "potential conflict" (Fligstein, 129) with each other.

Three explanations for this suggest themselves.

First, different concepts of identity apply to different "social fields", as Fligstein (128) puts it. This means that they are constituted by different levels of social interaction and, accordingly, also affect different levels of social identification.

Second, even if different identities overlap or coincide, they can, at times, be seen as "nested or embedded" in each other. European identity can, for instance, be embedded in national identities.

Third, multiple identities are not necessarily going to be in conflict with each other, because, depending on the precise situation and circumstances, we normally decide how much importance and which priority to ascribe to each single identity in the given moment without actually having to *dismiss* any of them.

Although one identity, depending on the context, will be the dominant one in terms of priority, and therefore determine our interests and actions, this does not mean that other identities are *extinct* in that very moment. They are just *less important*. This shows that coexisting and overlapping identities are nothing extraordinary and that they thereby cover common ground despite involving different perspectives. However, if identities are situational, this implies that they can, under certain conditions, become competitive in terms of the priority ascribed to them, since they are manifestations of loyalties to different groups. In terms of these loyalties, the interests and objectives evoked by identities can—in confrontation with other concepts of identity, through the "dialectics of intolerance" (Kizilurek 1998, 33), as well as their (ab)use by external actors—indeed come into conflict (Sen 2006, 34). It is when being pushed to its limits or somehow endangered—no matter with what degree of certainty the threat is assessed as real (or imagined)—that identity becomes even more important and fundamentally relevant.

Coexisting, overlapping, competing and conflicting identities are of great importance in the case of *Cyprus*, an island in the Eastern Mediterranean at the crossroads of three continents. From time immemorial Cyprus has been the focus of various foreign powers competing for sovereignty—and (effectively) leaving the islanders struggling for identity. After more than three centuries of Ottoman rule, during which a Muslim population was introduced into the island, which had before mostly been inhabited by people of Greek-Orthodox persuasion, Cyprus became a British colony in 1878 and remained under British sovereignty until 1959. The independence Cyprus was granted, however, was limited insofar that Britain, Greece and Turkey became guarantor powers and were, under certain circumstances, given the right to intervene. Also, independence did not comply with the aims of either the Greek (Cypriot) or the Turkish (Cypriot) nationalist movements, who put up a violent fight for Enosis (union of Cyprus with Greece) and Taksim (partition of the island) respectively between the 1930s and 1950s.

The unwanted, bi-communal Republic of Cyprus was declared to have failed only three years after independence when, as a consequence of the Greek Cypriot attempt to alter state matters in their favor, hostilities between the Greek Cypriot and the Turkish Cypriot community broke out and the retreat into largely monoethnic enclaves began. When the Greek junta, supported by the National Guard, launched a *coup d'état* against President Makarios in July 1974 in order to force through Enosis, Turkey made use of its right to intervene and launched a two-stage invasion. The second phase, during which the Turkish army conquered almost 36 per cent of the island's territory, was widely considered illegal. As a consequence, the Turkish Cypriot state that came into being in the aftermath of this military operation and was, in 1983, declared to be the Turkish Republic of Northern Cyprus (TRNC) remains internationally unrecognized. The physical partition brought about in 1974 lasted until 2003, when, under immense pressure from the Turkish Cypriots, the Turkish Cypriot leadership gave in and announced the opening of the borders. This, however, did not lead to the reunification of the island. In 2004, both Cypriot communities voted on the United Nations' so-called Annan Plan, which was designed to found a United Cyprus Republic, in separate referenda: While the Turkish Cypriot community resoundingly accepted the Annan Plan, the Greek Cypriots just as strongly voted against it, so that, as of May 1st, 2004, the divided island became a member of the European Union but with the *acquis communautaire* being suspended in the Turkish Cypriot community.

The conflict which has gradually evolved in Cyprus over the centuries can, among other ways of categorizing it, be defined as one of conflicting identities. Symbols of these identities are displayed all over the island. Visitors are made aware of this by the profusion of flags, representing national, ethnic and cultural identities, by the churches and mosques, museums and statues, that are architectural manifestations of religious and historical identities, by the ever present auditory reminders of the different languages spoken on the island, reflecting diverse linguistic identities. In Cyprus, different concepts of identity are closely interlinked, and they are often defined in opposition to a counterpart in the respective other part of the island. Wherever you happen to be, you are made constantly aware of identity.

I should like to outline seven concepts of identity—national, ethnic, cultural, religious, linguistic, historical and European—which may be held to constitute core layers of culture, and consider their significance with regard to Cyprus, but also the constraints that they impose and the problems that they may lead to.

National Identity

FLAGS AS SYMBOLS of *national identity* are omnipresent in Cyprus. Other symbols of this concept of identity that one comes across are passports, indicating citizenship, national holidays and national anthems. In the case of Cyprus, all these symbols illustrate its position in a polygon of national identities.

Karl Deutsch (1953) described national identity as follows:

> National identity is a peculiar kind of identity that implies that a group of people decide on some bases of pre-existing solidarities to express its collective identity in the context of creating a state to enforce rules to preserve that identity (16).

To him, national identity was an agreement, a decision, a will of a people to found its own nation state, which would, once created, ensure the protection of national identity. Weichlein (2006, 8) highlights the same point—national identity is based on the phenomenon of nationalism, and its formation can, accordingly, be traced back to the end of the eighteenth century at the earliest. Eickelpasch / Rademacher (73) point out that national identity comes into being through the (violent) exercise of power, since the unity of the nation, which is not natural, has to be secured in a dual process: first, in a negative way, by the suppression of cultural differences and, second, in a positive way, by the creation of national discourses, narratives and a shared version of the nation's history—the interlinkage between national and historical identity is undeniable. National identity, which is tied to the idea of a national territory (71), is often said to be the most powerful, fundamental and inclusive form of collective identity (68, see also Smith 1991, 143). This means that, although a coexistence of national and other identities is indeed possible, national identity will always dominate other concepts of identity and will, therefore, be the primary source of identity for most people (Wehler 2001, 36). Jansen / Borggräfe (2007, 19 f.) explain that this is the "dogma of nationalism", and, therefore, loyalty towards one's nation will always prevail over other loyalties for ethical reasons.

In the case of Cyprus, one has to distinguish between two different forms of national identity: First, we are dealing with national identities that Cypriots officially acquired, which were superimposed on them by foreign powers. This is true of their belonging in former times to the Ottoman Empire, of their British citizenship after 1914, after the island had become a Crown Colony, and of their status as citizens of the newly founded Republic of Cyprus after 1960; also, although internationally not recognized, of some of them being citizens of the TRNC. Second, we are confronted with those national identities which Cypriots have either (violently) fought for in the past, which are either Greek or Turkish, or which they have adopted comparatively recently, namely Greek Cypriot and Turkish Cypriot identities. The Greek and Turkish national identities that the Cypriots strove for so enthusiastically and determinedly between 1930 and 1959 in nationalist movements had initially been imported to the island from Greece and Turkey respectively. The nationalist aims of Enosis and Taksim can be seen as decisive forces in the making of Cypriot history, since, ultimately, the persistent desire for Enosis led to the 1974 *coup d'état* and the subsequent Turkish invasion, which, strictly speaking, made Taksim become a *de facto* reality.

The events of 1974 gave rise to feelings of betrayal and

abandonment by their motherland among the Greek Cypriots (Stamatakis 1991), which led to a decline of the Greek national identity and, gradually, to the evolution of a distinct Greek Cypriot identity and a reemphasis, a reinvention and a revival of the Republic of Cyprus, which henceforth no longer included the Turkish Cypriots. This Greek Cypriot identity was further strengthened after the referenda on the Annan Plan in 2004, since apparently there was no need to maintain strong ties with mother Greece and the Greek Cypriots had successfully preserved their Republic. However, the Greek Cypriots' sense of identity, with its switching of emphasis to either the *Greek* or the *Cypriot* momentum, depending on whom they need to distinguish themselves from, could certainly be described as conflicted (Faustmann 2009, 22).

In the Turkish Cypriot community, on the other hand, we have witnessed, after 1974 and even more so after 1983, when the climax of the Turkish Cypriot nationalism of 1974 was reached, a gradual identity transformation from a dominant Turkish national identity to a distinct, independent and self-determined Turkish Cypriot identity, which became stronger the more the Turkish Cypriots felt left behind by their Turkish motherland (Lacher / Kaymak 2005, 158). This national identity was clearly voiced in the 2003 mass protests against the regime in Northern Cyprus. The Turkish Cypriots' vote in the 2004 referendum in favor of the island's reunification and accession to the EU was the ultimate indication that Turkish nationalism among the Turkish Cypriots had irreversibly imploded (150). However, some scholars claim that, in much the same way as the Greek Cypriots, the Turkish Cypriots are trapped in an identity crisis: on the one hand, they perceive themselves to be Turkish Cypriot and increasingly less Turkish, while, on the other hand, they are apparently not Cypriot enough to overcome cultural differences with the Greek Cypriots so that, from the Greek Cypriots' point of view, they can be seen as compatriots in a future, reunified Cypriot state (Ramm 2005, 11).

Ethnic Identity

IN ADDITION TO national identity, the concept of *ethnic identity* is the most widely-used concept of identity in the discourse on Cypriot identities. Ethnic identity is in any case probably the most debated concept as far as its initial meaning and origins are concerned (Ganguly 2009, xvii). In the past, ethnic identity was often considered as "quasi-natural" (*quasi-natürlich*, Eder 2006, 37) and constituted by biological factors (Fearon / Laitin 2000, 98). According to Fought (2006), "the term 'ethnicity' was used as if it were the socially defined counterpart to the biologically defined 'race'" (4). From a constructivist point of view, this "primordialist" perception is to be rejected. Today, most scholars would agree on the basic assertion that ethnic identity is, in fact, founded on the shared belief in a real, or fictitious, common descent (Leggewie 1996, 50). Opinions on how and by what this common descent is represented differ strongly, however. While, in this respect, some scholars, like, for example, Carmen Fought, point to the importance of culture and history, others highlight a common religion as unifying the group. Others claim that it is "common language which binds members of an ethnic group together and allows them to communicate with each other" (Ganguly 2009). Max Weber's definition of ethnicity includes all of the previously mentioned points. He regards "perceptions of common descent/history/ fate and culture, which usually refers to some mix of language, physical appearance, and the ritual regulation of life, especially religion" as central features of a community bound by its ethnic identity (cited in Hale 2004, 141). Smith (1993) suggests "the sense of attachment to a particular land, the fervently held belief in an historical connection of this people with that land" (298) as another criterion for ethnicity. In this respect, it is not "the possession of the homeland, but the sense of mutual belonging, even from afar" (*ibid.*) that makes the difference. All in all, the variety of definitions of ethnic identity illustrates the complexity of the subject and the risk of blurred concepts of identities, since aspects of cultural, religious, linguistic and historical identity flow into the definitions of ethnic identity.

In Cyprus, the concept of ethnic identity acquired significance during the transitional period from Ottoman to British colonial rule. The Tanzımat reforms of 1839, 1856 and 1864, which were originally aimed at preserving the integrity of the Ottoman Empire, diminished the role of religious identities by "[granting legal] equality to all individuals, regardless of their religion"; they thereby "opened all spheres to [the] diverse groups" (Yavuz 1991, 65), triggering political competition among the Cypriots of both communities. "This competition took ethnic form" (66). Yavuz concludes that "[by] 1878 [...] the basis of the *millet* [system] had shifted to somewhere between religion and ethnicity". The new, decisive role that ethnic identity soon fully assumed could also be detected in connection with Greece's influence on the Greek-Orthodox education system, which was, after the foundation of the Greek state, organized along the lines of Hellenism (Apeyitou 2003, 75).

Cultural Identity

TURNING NOW TO the concept of *cultural identity*, it is hard to overlook the fact that "culture" has probably been one of the most discussed terms of recent years, with scholars from all over the world making their individual contributions, working towards a broadly acceptable definition, anatomizing its elements, using it as an explanation for all sorts of misunderstandings, and highlighting its importance, but also its constraints. Without trying to add to the debate, I will, within the scope of this essay, stick to Hofstede's (1991) anthropological definition of culture as "'the collective programming of the mind that distinguishes the members of one group or category of people from others" (4). He refers to Sumner's theory of *in-* and *out-groups*, with an in-group being "a cohesive group that offers protection in exchange for loyalty and provides its members with a sense of identity" (401). Robins (1996, 79) also emphasizes that cultural identities have to be dealt with in terms of cultural relationships. He writes that "it [is] only through the others that we become aware of who we are and what we stand for" (79).

But it is not only the term culture that is much talked about—it comes as no surprise to discover that the concept of *cultural identity* has been equally controversial. In *The Illusion of Cultural Identity* (1996), Jean-François Bayart sets out to expose cultural identity and other concepts of identity as mere constructs, crediting them with political, ideological and/or historical motivations (ix). He links culture with such ideas as "myth" (11), "instrumentalization of tradition" (38), and "recent innovation" (11). In his opinion, cultural identity cannot adequately explain political or economic actions (12). He concludes that "it is not certain that the 'cultural reason' that we all think we depend upon actually determines our actions, or even that it exists as a totality or a tangible system" (9). Nor does Bayart believe that human beings identify themselves mainly in terms of membership of a culture, but rather "with respect to the communities and cultures with which [they] have relations" (95), identities being defined much more in relation to each other than in themselves and in connection with their own doctrines.

Bayart's criticism indeed seems highly justified with regard to Cypriot identities, which are always defined in relation to an invisible counterpart on the other side of the island. Although both Cypriot communities always did and still do remain distinct with regard to, for example, their national identities, common cultural features evolved during the centuries of coexistence. To put it differently, the cultural identities of Greek Cypriots and Turkish Cypriots certainly coincided in a number of areas, and many of these similarities still exist today. However, they, and with them the possible basis for the evolution of a common Cypriot identity, run the risk of falling into oblivion the longer the division between the two communities persists. Moreover, the question as to how strong the *British* influence on Cypriot cultural identities was was raised when, after the British had taken over the island's administration in 1878, the education of Muslim Cypriots became largely dependent on the British rulers since the Ottoman Empire was, according to the Cyprus Convention of 1878, no longer allowed to take care of it and the Turkish motherland had not yet come into being (Apeyitou, 75, and Attalides 1979, 42). The Muslim Cypriots consequently ran the risk of losing their cultural identity due to becoming intensely anglicized (Choisi 1993, 11). The question as to how the legacy of British colonial rule should be dealt with still seems relevant today.

Religious Identity

WITH THE "imagined kinships" (Mitchell 2006, 191) that it creates, *religious identity* is a concept represented in Cyprus by religious practices, buildings such as churches and mosques, flags, and various symbols like, for instance, the Christian Cross or the Islamic Star and Crescent. This shows that religious identities are "based on alignments of culture and its elements—values, symbols, myths and traditions, often codified in custom and ritual" (Smith 1991, 6). However, religious identities overlap not only with the concept of cultural identity but also with ethnic identities, since "most religious communities [coincide] with ethnic groups" (*ibid.*), which is very true in the case of Cyprus.

Although religious minorities have always been present in Cyprus, the main focus was, and still is, on the coexistence of Christianity and Islam. Looking at Cyprus' history before the island was taken over by the British necessarily draws attention to the significance of these two religious identities. Joseph (2004, 172) reminds us that "[in] Europe, for over 1000 years beginning in the fourth century after Christ, religion was the primary focus of people's identity". Religion was omnipresent and permeated all spheres of life. Its strength lay in the fact that it tackles basic human concerns by providing answers to such questions as where we come from and where we are going.

Religion is concerned with "our entire existence, not just the moment to moment" (*ibid.*), and "can provide spiritual resources to explain and justify circumstances and events" (Mitchell, 196).

Cyprus' Christian heritage stands out due to the belief that it was Apostle Barnabas' place of burial, which was discovered in Cyprus in 600 AD. "[Since] then, the archbishops of Cyprus have been discovered [*sic*] direct descendants of Apostle Barnabas" (Choisi 1995, 35). The Church of Cyprus was attached to the Byzantine Empire and Orthodox Christianity in 395 AD, and Cyprus remained a Byzantine province until the arrival of Richard the Lionheart in 1191—a historical fact still illustrated today by the flying of the Byzantine flag next to Greek-Orthodox churches.

Through the Ottoman conquest of Cyprus in 1570-71 and the subsequent settlement there of people from Anatolia, Islam found its way onto the island. Under Ottoman rule, the administration and the extent of autonomy granted to Non-Muslim religious communities were matters regulated by the so-called *millet* system. The fact that the Greek-Orthodox archbishop was allowed to rule over the Greek-Orthodox Cypriots in 1754 made religious identity henceforth coincide with political and administrative functions and, albeit to a more limited extent, power. The differentiation of religious identity also served as the basis for the empire's legal system. For instance, the question of who was allowed to marry whom was regulated by law, and in terms of religious affiliation (Joseph, 172).

Generally speaking, although religion has often been more resistant to social change than other indicators of identity (see Mitchell, 193), it was profoundly challenged by the Age of Enlightenment, whose end coincided with the birth of nationalism, which then again gave birth to national identities as a new primary source of identity. But since national identities in Cyprus did not develop as early as in other parts of Europe, and because of the Ottoman *millet* system, which had institutionalized religion, religious identities were able to retain their dominance longer than in the rest of Europe.

Today, according to the *CIA World Factbook* (2010), 78 per cent of Cyprus' population is Greek-Orthodox and 18 per cent is of Muslim belief. Since the Church of Cyprus was deprived of its political power after Makarios' death in 1977, its influence has been limited to the private sphere, where it is, however, still very important. The celebration of name days and other religious festivities is just one illustration of this. In contrast, although Islam is the common religious faith in Northern Cyprus, its practice seems to be less strict than in many parts of the Turkish motherland. This, for instance, is evident from the fact that it is mostly settler women who wear headscarves, and not the Turkish Cypriot women (see Ramm, 10).

Linguistic Identity

BECAUSE OF DIGLOSSIA, *linguistic identity* in Cyprus is a diverse matter. In each of the two Cypriot communities, we are faced at the very least with a linguistic triangularism: Within the Greek Cypriot community, this triangularism is constituted by the Greek Cypriot dialect, Standard Modern Greek, and English as a legacy of British colonial rule. Although English is not officially recognized as a *lingua franca* (McEntee-Atalianis 2004, 81), but instead learned as a second or foreign language (Karoulla-Vrikki 1991, 50), it permeates all spheres of everyday life, so that some scholars speak of the evolution of a "kind of creole'" language (Ioannou 1991, 28), a hybrid linguistic identity that is developing due to the increasing influence of English. The overall linguistic situation in the Republic of Cyprus is also being made more complex by the growing spread of Asian languages, of Russian and Arabic.

The Turkish Cypriot community, on the other hand, is faced with the interplay of Cypriot Turkish, Standard Turkish and the diverse Anatolian dialects. With the settlement of mainland Turks in Northern Cyprus after 1974, a process of linguistic exchange was initiated which gave rise to first indicators of a hybrid linguistic identity, namely a mixture of Cypriot Turkish with elements from Standard Turkish (Demir / Johanson 2006). This hybrid form of identity is limited in terms of the linguistic phenomena concerned and the people who are affected, so that Cypriot Turkish remains the dominant language variety in Northern Cyprus.

A language, according to the eighteenth-century German historian and philosopher Herder, not only provides its speakers with a *personal* linguistic identity, but also creates a *collective* linguistic identity, one which is shared by all its speakers (see Weichlein 2006, 10). The thereby created "communities of speech" (Deutsch 1966, 41) that we are dealing with in the case of Cyprus are relatively small, quite distinct and geographically limited, both the Greek Cypriot dialect and Cypriot Turkish being linguistic varieties whose use is confined to the island, as well as by Cypriot emigrants living elsewhere in the world (Karoulla-Vrikki, 44). By speaking a dialect as their native language, these communities of speech develop and strengthen a linguistic identity that is distinct from that of standard language speakers. However, the use of a native language constitutes only one, albeit the primary, "layer of linguistic identity", one which is usually credited with generating a special emotional attachment (Joseph, 185). Other layers of linguistic identity come into play when speaking the (non-native) standard language or a second language. This illustrates the flexibility that this concept of identity offers, since the adaptation to different (linguistic) contexts is facilitated by the switching between languages.

It is important to acknowledge that the current linguistic *status quo* is always subject to change: Whatever attempts to preserve a language may be undertaken, for instance through language institutes or dictionaries, or by using it as a means of education, languages, and consequently linguistic identity too, are continuously changing (Deutsch, 44), since they are influenced by the pluralistic world that they are used in. This also includes the effects of globalization and migration, which are increasingly challenging linguistic identities.

Historical Identity

THE CONCEPT OF *historical identity* is based on Maurice Halbwachs' theory of collective memory (*mémoire collective*) which he defines as "a socially constructed notion" (Coser 1992, 22) working within frameworks "[which are] used by [the members of a social group in order] to determine and retrieve their recollections" (Coser, 43). Although it is the individual group members that remember, the frames for and limits of this memory are provided by the group that they belong to— Halbwachs uses the term *cadres sociaux* (cited in Assmann 1992, 35). Collective memory fulfills the human need to feel embedded in the flow of time, to feel rooted and part of society, its history and its continuity. What Halbwachs calls collective memory, in fact, constitutes the core of historical identity, since it positions us in a group's perception of the past and present and therefore in the group's historical identity. Thus, a community of shared fate is created (Eickelpasch / Rademacher, 69), in which every individual's historical identity is inseparably fastened to the group's historical identity. Commemorative events, national celebrations and holidays, as well as particular locations such as buildings, statues or memorials, are symbols and visible manifestations of this historical identity (Assmann, 38 f.).

Assmann (36) rightly points out that Halbwachs' theory of collective memory not only explains the process of remembering, but also the process of forgetting. Only what can be reconstructed, and therefore remembered and commemorated within a group and its social frames, is part of the collective memory. Events which are not communicated and talked about are denied those social frames and will consequently be forgotten (37). Furthermore, according to Halbwachs, "[everything] that might separate individuals will, as well, be erased from the collective memory" (Coser, 182 f.). In the sense that collective memory, and therefore the historical identity constituted by it, is selective, it constructs and "invents" history and the group believing in it (Kizilurek 1999, 387).

All of this illustrates the point that Niethammer (2000, 352) is making when he says that one cannot speak of "objective remembrance of the past", since it is evident that the processes of remembering and forgetting are socially constructed. Taking historical identity as a social construct not only provides us with the means of analyzing its mechanisms, it also leads us to the question of how it is communicated to others. Not only do we make the collective memory available to other groups *not* sharing the same historical recollections, we also ensure a passing on of our historical identity to our offspring. Children will, through the process of socialization, grow into the national memory and thereby be drawn with a "feeling of temporal embeddedness into the collective march of history" (Eickelpasch / Rademacher, 69). In addition to the narration of history in a family context, this can also be achieved through the education offered in schools (Assmann, 51 ff.). Evaluating education in terms of how nationalist aspirations and ideologies are conveyed, which indicates the strong linkage between historical and national identity, is particularly interesting. John Stuart Mill in his *Considerations on Representative Government* (1861) noted the bonds between historical and national identity:

> T[he] feeling of nationality may have been generated by various causes. Sometimes it is the effect of identity of race and descent. Community of language, and community of religion, greatly contribute to it. Geographical limits are one of its causes. *But the strongest of all is identity of political antecedents; the possession of a national history, and consequent community of recollections; collective pride and humiliation, pleasure and regret, connected with the same incidents in the past* (chapter 16, my emphasis).

Ernest Renan adopts a similar point of view in his 1882 lecture *What Is a Nation?*, declaring that the core of a nation is formed by "a rich heritage of memories [...] a heritage of glory and of grief to be shared [...] to have suffered, rejoiced and hoped together", *etc.* (153). But Deutsch (19) points out that a heritage of memories will only unite people if they are already united in another way, for instance by nationality. If they are not, they might have *witnessed* the same historical events, but they will not *share* them since they will look at them from different, maybe opposing, points of view.

Since, in the context of the Cyprus conflict, reconstructions of the past have played such an important role, the concept of historical identity is decisive for the Cypriots of both communities. The historical identities of both communities still differ strongly because different historical events are anchored as core ones in the respective national memories. Similarly, different events have been selectively obliterated. The distinct national, historical memories of the Greek and the Turkish Cypriots are, for instance, kept alive through representation and commemoration in history text books at school, in museums, and at national celebrations.

The opening of the Cypriot borders in 2003 highlighted the different and distinct paths of historical identity that the two communities had been embarked on since the division in 1974: After 29 years of separation, the Greek Cypriots crossed the Green Line in search of the past, while the Turkish Cypriots did so in search of a future (Bose 2007, 60).

European Identity

THE TERM *European identity* denotes a collective, supranational concept of identity, politically bound to the European Union, which, in its recent form, came into being through the Treaty of Maastricht in 1992. I use the concept in a cultural, social, and political sense and thereby make allowance for the interlinkage between European and cultural identity.

Visible symbols of European identity include, for example, the flag of the European Union, its anthem, its common currency, the Euro, as well as the passports issued by the EU member states, which share particular design features (Fligstein, 125).

"[The concept of European identity] has become intensely politicized in recent years", as Checkel / Katzenstein put it (2009, 11). In an *inward*-looking discourse, the EU member states are constantly trying to identify their European "soul" (11), their "lowest common denominator". Yet "the [European] Union has not yet succeeded in crafting a common European sense of 'who we are'" (1). There is also an *outward*-looking aspect to the debate about European identity when the question about Europe's borders is raised—can they be defined according to geographical or cultural terms, or are they are based on a shared history? Defining Europe's borders also serves the purpose of differentiating it from other parts of the world. In Robins' words, "[the] positivity of European culture [is] defined against the negative image of 'non-Europe'" (Robins, 81), of the "Other". According to Huntington's theory of the clash of civilizations (1996), the Western world distinguishes itself from other civilizations through sharing certain core values, whereby the main difference to the (non-Western) out-groups is constituted by religion. Assuming that Huntington is right about the conflict potential between different civilizations—and Huntington's theory is still very controversial—the question has to be asked whether Cyprus, an intersection between the civilizational worlds of Orthodoxy and Islam, belongs to the West at all.

If you adopt an outsider's perspective on the EU, Europeans indisputably seem similar, but from the inside they are very distinct, and national identities are still strong in comparison with any feeling of a common "Europeanness"—also, because the latter is a rather young concept of identification. Münch (1999, 471) argues that a slight detachment from your national identity is required in order to enable any attachment to a supra-national identity. Checkel / Katzenstein call this the "positive-sum nature" of European identity (9): European identity can complement your national identity, and Cypriots, for instance, can so be and feel Cypriot and European at the same time. Münch (477) even takes it one step further by emphasizing that national identity "does not necessarily have to diminish to the same extent that European identity increases", but that instead a general "identity growth" (*Identitätswachstum*) can be observed.

According to Fligstein (126), the creation of a European identity can only happen through interaction between the European peoples, and not in isolation. These interactions, whether media-based or face-to-face, create bonds between them "that suggest that these people are more alike than different and hence, Europeans". Planting this feeling of a common Europeanness will be more successful the more cosmopolitan people are and, therefore, the "less national in their identities" (129). Fligstein (147, 156) and Münch (471, 473) agree that European identity, however, often proves to be a phenomenon of the elite, that is, the orientation towards a European identity increases with rising levels of education, salaries and job positions, since the number of opportunities for interaction with other Europeans is then significantly greater. However, a European identity can only be successfully built if, according to Münch (480), the commitment to this concept of identity does not remain a mere lip service, but results in concrete action. Being European involves more than just exercising your rights as European citizens, since there are duties to be fulfilled, too.

The location of Cyprus at a geographical and cultural cross-roads (Diez 2005, 301) raises the question of the relevance of the concept of European identity for the island. This is not something which suddenly became significant when the Republic of Cyprus applied for accession to the European Union in 1990— because of Cyprus' European historical and ideological heritage, it has been a matter of interest for the Cypriots for a long time. The referenda results of 2004 enabled the Greek Cypriots to finally and *officially* assume a European identity by becoming citizens of the EU, while the outcome of the referenda left the Turkish Cypriots with an unfulfilled longing for it.

In the long run, the EU could, however, provide "an all encompassing identity that [has] the potential to overcome the ethnic divide between Greek-Cypriots and Turkish-Cypriots" (Trimikliniotis 2007, 405) so that the stalemate caused by conflicting identities would be overcome. A European framework would then also provide the security the Cypriots might be afraid of losing when they detach themselves a little from their distinct Greek or Turkish Cypriot identities.

A FINAL NOTE on the state of identities in Cyprus: In the past, the Greek Cypriot and the Turkish Cypriot communities, forming the opposing parties in the Cyprus conflict, were each united in congruent concepts of identity. These identities were highly politicized—by external powers—and then used to legitimize and achieve political goals (Faiz 2003). The antagonism between the communities, and therefore also between their respective identities, was strengthened by the confrontation with the respective "Other". This means that not only were antagonistic identities fostered and preserved by the conflict (Choisi 1993, 15), but also the other way around, which further complicated the achieving of a solution to the conflict. However, this bipolar identity system provided the Cypriots of both communities with a feeling of security and a framework of orientation in the conflict. Clearly defining identities and their boundaries seems to be of particular importance in, and for, Cyprus, because of the numerous external influences and interventions that the island has been exposed to in the course of its history.

References

Apeyitou, Eleni. "Turkish-Cypriot Nationalism: Its History and Development (1571-1960)." In: *Cyprus Review*, 15, 1, 2003, 67-98.

Assmann, Jan. *Das kulturelle Gedächtnis: Schrift, Erinnerung und politische Identität in frühen Hochkulturen* (1992). Sixth edition. Munich: Beck, 2007.

Attalides, Michael. *Cyprus: Nationalism and International Politics* (1979). Mannheim: Bibliopolis, 2003.

Baumeister, Roy F. *Identity: Cultural Change and the Struggle for Self.* New York: Oxford University Press, 1986.

Bausinger, Hermann. *Kulturelle Identität.* Bonn: Deutsche UNESCO-Kommission, 1982.

Bayart, Jean-François. *The Illusion of Cultural Identity* [*L'Illusion Identitaire*, 1996]. London: Hurst, 2005.

Bose, Sumantra. *Contested Lands: Israel-Palestine, Kashmir, Bosnia, Cyprus, and Sri Lanka.* Cambridge, MA: Harvard University Press, 2007.

Checkel, Jeffrey T. / Katzenstein, Peter J. "The politicization of European identities." In: *European Identity.* Ed. Jeffrey T. Checkel / Peter J. Katzenstein. Cambridge: Cambridge University Press, 2009, 1-28.

Choisi, Jeanette. *Wurzeln und Strukturen des Zypernkonfliktes 1878 bis 1990: Ideologischer Nationalismus und Machtbehauptung im Kalkül konkurrierender Eliten.* Stuttgart: Franz Steiner, 1993.

------------. "The Greek Cypriot Élite—Its Social Function and Legitimization." In: *Cyprus Review*, 7, 1, 1995, 34-68.

CIA World Factbook, 2010: Cyprus. Website, <No longer online>

Coser, Lewis A. *Maurice Halbwachs: On Collective Memory.* Chicago: University of Chicago Press, 1992.

Demir, Nurettin / Johanson, Lars. "Dialect Contact in Northern Cyprus." In: *International Journal of the Sociology of Language*, 181, 2006, 1-9.

Deutsch, Karl W. *Nationalism and Social Communication: An Inquiry into the Foundations of Nationality* (1953). Second edition. Cambridge, MA: The MIT Press, 1966.

Diez, Thomas. "Eine doppelte Grenzproblematik: Zypern und die Europäische Union." In: *Grenzüberschreitungen: Differenz und Identität im Europa der Gegenwart.* Ed. Holger Huget / Chryssoula Kambas / Wolfgang Klein. Wiesbaden: VS Verlag für Sozialwissenschaften, 2005, 289-306.

Eder, Klaus. "Ethnien, Nationen, Zivilisationen, Interkulturalität." In: *Interkulturell denken und handeln:*

Theoretische Grundlagen und Orientierung für die gesell-schaftliche Praxis. Ed. Hans Nicklas / Burkhard Müller / Hagen Kordes. Bonn: bpb, 2006, 37-46.

Eickelpasch, Rolf / Rademacher, Claudia. *Identität*. Bielefeld: Transcript, 2004.

Faiz, Muharrem. "Cypriotness Today—Basis for a Multi-cultural Future for Cyprus." In: *Culture in Common—Living Cultures in the Cypriot Communities. Proceedings of German-Cypriot Forum Conference in Berlin* / Üdersee, 22nd-24th May, 2003. Website, <No longer online>

Faustmann, Hubert. "Aspects of Political Culture in Cyprus." In: *The Government and Politics of Cyprus*. Ed. James Ker-Lindsay / Hubert Faustmann. Bern: Peter Lang, 2009.

Fearon, James / Laitin, David D. "Violence and the Social Construction of Ethnic Identity" (2000). In: *Ethnic Conflict*. Ed. Rajat Ganguly. Volume I, 95-128.

------------ / Wendt, Alexander. "Rationalism v. Constructivism: A Skeptical View." In: Walter Carlsnaes / Thomas Risse / Beth A Simmons. *Handbook of International Relations*. London: Sage, 2002, 52-72.

Fligstein, Neil. *Euroclash: The EU, European Identity, and the Future of Europe*. Oxford: Oxford University Press, 2008.

Fought, Carmen. *Language and Ethnicity*. Cambridge: Cambridge University Press, 2006.

Ganguly, Rajat. "Introduction." In: *Ethnic Conflict*. Volume I: *Ethnic Identity*. Ed. Rajat Ganguly. London: Sage, 2009.

Hale, Henry E. "Explaining Ethnicity" (2004). In: *Ethnic Conflict*. Ed. Rajat Ganguly. Volume I, 129-52.

Hofstede, Geert / Hofstede, Gert Jan. *Cultures and Organizations: Software of the Mind* (1991). Second edition. New York: McGraw-Hill, 2005.

Huntington, Samuel P. *The Clash of Civilizations and the Remaking of World Order* (1996). New York: Simon & Schuster, 2003.

Ioannou, Yiannis E. "Language, Politics and Identity: An Analysis of the Cypriot Dilemma." In: *Cyprus Review*, 3, 1,

1991, 15-41.

Jansen, Christian / Borggräfe, Henning. *Nation— Nationalität—Nationalismus*. Frankfurt/M.: Campus, 2007.

Joseph, John E. *Language and Identity: National, Ethnic, Religious*. Basingstoke, Hants.: Palgrave Macmillan, 2004.

Karoulla-Vrikki, Dimitra. "The Language of the Greek Cypriots Today: A Revelation of an Identity Crisis?" In: *Cyprus Review*, 3, 1, 1991, 42-58.

Kizilurek, Niazi. "The Politics of Separation and the Denial of Interdependence." In: *Cyprus Review*, 10, 2, 1998, 33-39.

------------ . "National Memory and Turkish-Cypriot Textbooks." In: *Internationale Schulbuchforschung*, 21, 4, 1999, 387-95.

Lacher, Hannes / Kaymak, Erol. "Transforming Identities: Beyond the Politics of Non-settlement in North Cyprus." In: *Mediterranean Politics*, 10, 2, 2005, 147-66.

Leggewie, Claus. "Ethnizität, Nationalismus und multikulturelle Gesellschaft." In: *Nationales Bewusstsein und kollektive Identität: Studien zur Entwicklung des kollektiven Bewusstseins in der Neuzeit 2*. Ed. Helmut Berding. Frankfurt/M.: Suhrkamp, 1996, 46-65.

McEntee-Atalianis, Lisa J. "The Impact of English in Postcolonial, Postmodern Cyprus." In: *International Journal of the Sociology of Language*, 168, 2004, 77-90.

Mill, John Stuart. *Considerations on Representative Government* (1861). University of Adelaide Library, 2010. Website, <http://ebooks.adelaide.edu.au/m/mill/john_stuart/m645r/>

Mitchell, Claire. "The Religious Content of Ethnic Identities" (2006). In: *Ethnic Conflict*. Ed. Rajat Ganguly. Volume I, 188-204.

Münch, Richard. "Europäische Identitätsbildung: Zwischen globaler Dynamik, nationaler und regionaler Gegenbewegung." In. *Identität und Moderne*. Ed. Herbert Willems / Alois Hahn. Frankfurt/M.: Suhrkamp, 1999, 465-86.

Niethammer, Lutz. *Kollektive Identität: Heimliche Quellen*

einer unheimlichen Konjunktur. Reinbek: Rowohlt, 2000.

Ramm, Christoph. "Construction of Identity beyond Recognized Borders: The Turkish Cypriot Community between Cyprus, Turkey and the European Union." European Studies Center, St. Antony's College, Oxford. Conference lecture, June 2005. Website, <http://www.sant.ox.ac.uk/esc/esc-lectures/ramm.pdf>

Renan, Ernest. "What Is a Nation?" ["Qu'est-ce qu'une nation?", 1882]. In: *The Nationalism Reader*. Ed. Omar Dahbour / Micheline R. Ishay. Atlantic Highlands, NJ: Humanities Press, 1995, 143-55.

Robins, Kevin. "Interrupting Identities: Turkey / Europe." In: *Questions of Cultural Identity*. Ed. Stuart Hall / Paul du Gay. London: Sage, 1996, 61-86.

Sen, Amartya. *Die Identitätsfalle: Warum es keinen Kampf der Kulturen gibt* [*Identity and Violence: The Illusion of Destiny*, 2006]. Bonn: bpb, 2007.

Smith, Anthony D. *National Identity*, Reno, NV: University of Nevada Press, 1991.

------------. "The Ethnic Sources of Nationalism" (1993). In: *Ethnic Conflict*. Ed. Rajat Ganguly. Volume I, 295-307.

Stamatakis, Nikos A. "History and Nationalism: The Cultural Reconstruction of the Modern Greek Cypriot Identity". In: *Cyprus Review*, 3, 1, 1991, 59-86.

Trimikliniotis, Nicos. "Nationality and Citizenship in Cyprus since 1945: Communal Citizenship, Gendered Nationality and the Adventures of a Post-colonial Subject in a Divided Country." In: *Citizenship Policies in the New Europe* (2007). Ed. Rainer Bauböck / Bernhard Perchinig / Wiebke Sievers. Expanded and updated edition. Amsterdam: Amsterdam University Press, IMISCOE Research, 2009, 389-418.

Ulbert, Cornelia. "Sozialkonstruktivismus." In: *Theorien der Internationalen Beziehungen*. Ed. Siegfried Schieder / Manuela Spindler. Second edition. Opladen: Verlag Barbara Budrich, 2006, 409-40.

Wehler, Hans-Ulrich. *Nationalismus: Geschichte, Formen,*

Folgen. Munich: C. H. Beck, 2001.

Weichlein, Siegfried. *Nationalbewegungen und Nationalismus in Europa.* Darmstadt: WBG, 2006.

Yavuz, M. Hakan. "The Evolution of Ethno-nationalism in Cyprus under the Ottoman and British Systems." In: *Cyprus Review*, 3, 2, 1991, 57-79.

LA BELLA FIGURA

Unlocking Italy's Not-So-Secret Social Grammar
by Anna Brünig

You have probably heard this before: *fare bella figura* can be crucial to one's success when in Italy, no matter whether you are travelling, doing business or living there. All the travel guides agree. What is not explained, however, is how to actually achieve *bella figura*. Apart from general advice such as "dress up and look your best", making a *bella figura* seems somewhat of a mystery. Or, even more probable, the authors think that that's all there is to it—that looking good is all it takes. In the following essay, however, I would like to define *bella figura* as a complex cultural phenomenon that encompasses all spheres of Italian social life. Attempts will be made to find its roots in Italian history and describe possible reasons why members of other cultures frequently fail to understand the true character of *figura*, associating it with dissimulation and insincerity.

So—what exactly does *bella figura* mean?

> *Il Nuovo Dizionario Italiano Garzanti* defines *far figura* as "*essere appariscente*" ("to be showy or striking, remarkable") and "*dare una buona impressione, apparire migliore della realtà*" ("to give a good impression, to appear better than the reality"). However, the term is usually construed as *far(e) bella figura*, literally: "to make a beautiful figure." (Note that sometimes the

final "*e*" of the infinitive "*fare*" is dropped.) Garzanti says *far bella figura* means "*riuscire bene, ottenere apprezzamento e stima*" ("to succeed well; to obtain appreciation and respect"). Its opposite exists as well, namely *fare brutta figura*, literally "to make an ugly figure". There is also *fare cattiva figura*, in which *cattiva* translates as "bad", a slightly stronger indictment than *brutta*. [...] Interestingly, if no adjective is used for *figura*, *bella* is intended. For example, to simply *far figura* means to look good. Sometimes, though, the negative tone of an utterance can substitute for an adjective in carrying the message of *brutta*. *Che figura che ho fatto!* ("What a figure I made!") said in a tone of dismay implies a catastrophe (Nardini 1999, 8 f.).

Giovanna Del Negro (2004) explains that

> *Bella figura* is largely measured in terms of demeanor and presentational style. Attire, grooming, posture, physical grace, manners, and conversational skills are carefully monitored and judged. While expensive clothing is valued, one need not be wealthy to cut a fine figure. It is better to walk with a smooth gait and wear a pleasing combination of simple clothes than to slouch about in designer fashions or wear expensive garments that are ill-fitting or poorly coordinated. One's clothing, gait, and demeanor mark one as respectable, or ill mannered (131 f.).

Not only does being wealthy not guarantee *bella figura*, it can even be the other way around: purchasing stylish and budget-friendly items is very *en vogue*. In magazines, entire issues are dedicated to this trend called *cheap&chic*, explaining how to *essere glam anche in tempo di crisi* ("be glamorous even in times of crisis"). During my fieldwork in a small village in northern Italy, a couple was admired for their idea of booking low-budget flight tickets for a number of close friends and having their stag and hen parties in Valencia, Spain, during the "Tomatina" festival. This idea seemed very new and exciting to all the lucky guests; at the same time, it did not entail having to spend an excessive amount of money (while still appearing generous). They certainly made *gran bella figura*.

The circumstances, however, can be of the utmost importance, as *figura* is relative. Had a different couple, at the same time, invited their guests to Hawaii or another exotic destination, they would have made even *più bella figura*—as generosity always pays off in terms of *figura*. Organizing an unforgettable event or ceremony but expecting the guests to pay for themselves, on the other hand, would be considered extremely rude and almost certainly result in a *brutta figura*.

Often, non-Italians tend to see the putting on of a *figura* as a form of deception, associating it with a cover-up, as if appearance, manners and staging were to triumph over substance. *Bella Italia* seems to be a nation where public impression management is at its most conscious and tactical. "While there is [...] always some level of artifice and impression management involved, to see *figura* as exclusively or even primarily put-on is to miss the point", claims Gloria Nardini (18), professor at the University of Illinois at Chicago and author of the only scholarly study of *bella figura*.

> Veracity, or the lack thereof, has nothing to do with anything in this case. [...] What all of these interpretations share is a peculiarly American naiveté which sees *figura* as somehow separate from the true self, the pristine, unadorned self. They fail to comprehend the very subtle, all-encompassing, and public ways in which the expression of Italian identity is imbricated in creating *bella figura*. Thus, those who ask, "Where is the real person behind the *bella figura*?" fail to understand the point: *bella figura* is a social construction of identity that depends upon public performance for

its reification. In its "interaction between personal aspiration and assessment by others" (Pitkin 1993, 98), it becomes part of the real person's creation and presentation of self. To oversimplify, the "real person" is *in* the *bella figura* (20).

I, TOO, HAVE FAILED many times to really understand *bella figura*. Even though I had heard my Italian friends use the expression over and over again, I wasn't able to use it properly for years. During my field studies, I would intentionally mention *bella* or *brutta figura* in my conversation and carefully monitor people's reactions, hoping that they would agree and consider my choice of words appropriate. Once, while buying ice-cream, I accidentally pushed to the front. As soon as I realized my mistake, I apologized and said "Mi dispiace! Che figuraccia!" Both the barista and the young man I had overlooked laughed, and answered: "Ah! Se le figuracce fossero queste...!", indicating that this was nothing, compared to a *real figuraccia*. I was confused and kept asking myself what a real *figuraccia* was, then. I came to the conclusion that my audience, consisting of only two individuals, had not considered my behavior deliberately rude and disrespectful, two main aspects of *brutta figura*—I therefore simply did not qualify for a *figuraccia*.

Another situation that did not seem to fit into my definition of *figura* was the fact that in Italy, too, people would dress poorly, wearing shabby clothes that I would not have dared be seen in. This is certainly a point that travel guides do not stress: even though the country is world famous for expensive designer fashion, the streets are actually full of normal-looking people. My friend Elena, for example, works as a kindergarten teacher in a small, rather sleepy village. During her work, she will take care of the children wearing cheap, worn pants and sweaters, and no makeup, and paying very little attention to her hairstyle. This used to puzzle me because her running around in public the way she did seemed to contradict even the simplest *figura* rules. When, one afternoon, I picked her up after work in order to spend the afternoon in a nearby shopping mall, she told me that we had to drive to her house first, saying: "Non ci posso andare così! Sono vestita malissima, anzi, sono indecente!" ("I can't go there like this! I am dressed awfully, I am indecent, rude!"). I realized that in Italy everything depends on the context and the audience: in her village, Elena had felt at ease because everybody knew that she was doing her job, which did not require perfect looks. The audience knew her well enough to see that this was not a sign of disrespect to the community. No signs of superficiality, here. As soon as the context changed and people would not know and respect her for what she did but judge by appearances, it became necessary to change her appearance in order to fit in.

To RETURN TO Gloria Nardini's study of the phenomenon:

> My contention is that *bella figura* is a central metaphor of Italian life, admittedly an extremely complicated one. It is a construct that refers to face, looking good, putting on the dog, style, appearance, flair, showing off, ornamentation, etiquette, keeping up with the Joneses, image, illusion, esteem, social status, reputation—in short, self-presentation and identity, performance and display. [...] As a cultural code, it is deeply embedded as one of the primary arbiters of Italian social mores, so deeply embedded that natives are frequently unaware (consciously at least) of conforming to it. But understanding Italian life is impossible without understanding the intensity with which one must *fare bella figura* or, even more importantly, avoid *brutta figura* (7).

For the anthropologist Sydel Silverman (1975):

> The concern with one's *bella figura* is ever-present as a quite self-conscious guide to behavior. The concept

is a measure of personal integrity, but it has little to do with one's essence, character, intention, or other inner condition, rather it centers upon public appearances. To acquire and preserve *bella figura* requires being impeccable before the eyes of others. Physically, one must be as immaculate and elegant as possible, if not at all times, given the necessities of work, then at least when engaging in social interaction after work. One must always present a pleasant face to the world, regardless of the negative emotions that may simmer behind it. [...] One must show oneself to be knowledgeable of the proper order of rights and obligations in social relations (40).

Bella figura has, above all, to do with respect: the individual's behavior has to be adapted to community values and expectations in order to preserve the proper order of things. This makes *bella figura* both a guide to correct conduct and a powerful social grammar: follow the unwritten rules and you will be respected and considered a worthy member of the community.

Closely linked to questions of respect is the concept of *face* with its key elements of *honor* and *shame*. More than four decades ago, J. G. Peristiany (1966) wrote:

Honor and shame are two poles of an evaluation. They are the reflection of the social personality in the mirror of social ideals. What is particular to these evaluations is that they use as standard of measurement the type of personality considered as representative and exemplary of a certain society. This way of reasoning can only lead to the conclusion that as all societies evaluate conduct by comparing it to ideal standards of action, all societies have their own forms of honor and shame. Indeed, they have. [...] When the individual emerges with a full social personality of his own, his honor is in his sole keeping. In this insecure, individualist, world where nothing is accepted on credit, the individual is constantly forced to prove and assert himself. Whether as the protagonist of his group or as a self-seeking individualist, he is constantly "on show", he is forever courting the public opinion of his "equals" so that they may pronounce him worthy (9 f.).

In Peristiany's words, the efforts of fare *bella figura* would thus be a means to "court the public opinion" in order to preserve one's honor.

> In Italy, specifically, *figura* can be thought of as encompassing both honor and shame. That is, *bella figura* represents "honor" (a word in most Italian contexts seldom mentioned) and *brutta figura* "shame" or *vergogna* (a word more frequently mentioned) (Nardini, 18).

Considering that manifestations of honor and shame vary from country to country, the historian Peter Burke (1987) speaks of "three Europes: north-western, southern, and eastern. Southern Europe, Mediterranean Europe, was Romance-speaking, Catholic [...] with an outdoor culture and a value-system laying great stress on honor and shame" (57). This value-system, however, remains difficult to understand for members of those cultures, mainly from north-western Europe (and North America) who have internalized the notion of self as an interior mechanism restrained by *guilt*, rather than *shame* (Nardini, 18).

Nardini's view of *bella figura* as a social construction of identity dependent upon public performance for its reification has already been quoted, and, as she says, "to figure means to make oneself be noticed. *Figura* is always linked to appearance. If one were to remain closed up in a room, *figura* would not count at all (10)". It is this essential link to public performance that causes misunderstandings: even though *bella figura* needs an audience, this does not necessarily mean that Italians are forever (consciously) acting as if they were on a stage—even if, to a stranger, it may seem like this.

As Lander MacClintock (1920) wrote many years ago:

> It is true that the Italians have by nature many gifts as actors, vivid, expressive faces, mobile, eloquent bodies, musical, flexible voices, the capacity for working themselves up to climaxes of passion, a hereditary tradition of great and clever acting. One can scarcely set foot in Italy without realizing that he is among a nation of actors (9).

Luigi Barzini, author of *The Italians: A Full-Length Portrait Featuring Their Manners and Morals* (1964), confirms that "This reliance on symbols and spectacles must be clearly grasped if one wants to understand Italy, Italian history, manners, civilization, and habits. It is the fundamental trait of the national character" (90). As such, it is deeply rooted in history, especially the Renaissance.

> We all act in public, and perhaps in private as well. However, some societies, in some periods, seem to encourage this style of behavior more than others, and the dramaturgical approach seems peculiarly appropriate to Italy in the early modern period, the age of the Renaissance and the Baroque. Italy was a "theatre society" (*società spettacolo*, Titone), where it was necessary to play one's social role with style, *fare bella figura*, to work hard at creating and maintaining as well as saving "face". There is of course a danger for a northerner of seeing Italian society in stereotyped terms [...]. In this aspect, Italy was and is part of the wider Mediterranean culture. [...] The Mediterranean world is a world where life (more exactly, male life) is lived in public, on the square, which is well adapted to both performance and observation (Burke, 9 f.).

Prototypical for early modern Italy's social ideals was Baldassare Castiglione's *Il Cortegiano*, translated into English by Sir Thomas Hoby as *The Courtier* in 1561, a book of etiquette that uses a set of examples which portray the ideal Renaissance man and woman. Written between 1513 and 1518, this treatise was inspired by a series of conversations among a group of aristocrats at the court of Urbino in 1507. Its central theme includes the nature of graceful behavior, especially the impression of effortlessness, or *sprezzatura*.

Sprezzatura, in turn, is one of the most important aspects of *bella figura*, meaning understated elegance and the complete absence of affectation. Nardini quotes Castiglione's famous words: "Therefore that may bee saide to be a verie arte, that appeareth not to be arte, neither ought a man to put more diligence in any thing than in covering it; [...]" (*The Courtier*, 46), and explains that Castiglione owes this idea of "a kind of artful grace which appears artless, [...] a studied carelessness, a nonchalant display which conceals the efforts expended to acquire it" (Nardini, 24) to Cicero's *Orator* and Ovid's *Art of Love*.

Nardini defines *sprezzatura* as follows:

> It is a derivative of the verb *sprezzare*, an alternate of *disprezzare* (to disdain), which means *non curare* (not to pay attention to) from the Vulgar Latin *expretiare* consisting of *pretium* (esteem) and *ex* (not). Therefore, the implication is that in order to achieve *sprezzatura*, one must act in a manner which accords little (ostensible) attention to one's actions (25 f.).

In Italian self-presentation and impression management, according to Del Negro (2004), the ideal performer

> should have a spontaneous and unselfconscious personal style. The term *disinvoltura* can be used interchangeably with *sprezzatura*. [...] Significantly,

disinvoltura is not achieved by marking social distinctions, but politely, recognizing others. To be *disinvolto,* performers must acknowledge that they are performing and others are paying attention to the performance, without drawing undue attention to either fact. [...] The difficulty for the actor, therefore, lies in looking natural and unaffected while at the same time abiding by the complex rules of etiquette and decorum (131 f.).

So, whether you are trying to be *disinvolto,* or to make *bella figura,* you must acknowledge other people's awareness appropriately, indicating that you are the object of public attention without pompously strutting like an actor on a stage: "Too much self-consciousness, and you are precious; too little, and you have pretensions of naïveté" (133).

WHILE IN MOST cultures, a certain degree of public impression management is considered a part of normal everyday behavior, Burke (1987) found substantial differences in the importance that is given to sincerity:

Goffman's metaphor of the theater of everyday life was intended to refer to everyone, not just the Italians. And yet... there is a significant contrast to be made between the cultural styles of northern and southern Europe, if only it can be made with more finesse and formulated in a less ethnocentric way. [...] The sociologist Norbert Elias described what he called the "threshold of embarrassment" in western civilization and the way in which it was raised over the centuries. In a similar manner, it might be useful to speak of a "sincerity threshold" which varies from one time and place to another. We might say that the sincerity threshold is higher in the West than (say) in China and Japan, and higher in northern Europe than in the south; and also that it has been raised at various times, notably the eighteenth century. It might be added that a kind of sliding scale operates, so that a stress on sincerity in a given culture tends to be associated with a lack of emphasis on other qualities, such as courtesy (12 f.).

In *sincerity cultures*, as Burke calls them, great stress is laid on authenticity, honesty and directness in communication. All too obvious acting and deceiving are regarded as highly threatening to social values and beliefs. Ever since the French Revolution, the peoples' favorite pastime seems to have been the unmasking of liars (and not only by means of lie-detector tests in talkshows on television). As Lionel Trilling (1972) puts it:

> The "unmasking trend" continues with unabated energy in our own time, and if we try to say why the idea that there is a mental system which lies hidden under the manifest system has won so wide an acceptance among us, doubtless one reason is that it accords with the firmly entrenched belief that beneath the appearance of every human phenomenon there lies concealed a discrepant actuality and that intellectual, practical, and (not least) moral advantage is to be gained by forcibly bringing it to light (141 f.).

The mistrust of suspiciously perfect manners and looks has a long tradition.

> It brings with it the idea that somewhere under all the roles there is Me, that poor old ultimate actuality, who, when all the roles have been played, would like to murmur "Off, off, you lendings!" and settle down with his own original actual self (10).

Elizabeth Burns (1972) argues that degrees of theatricality are culturally determined.

Most people like to think that sometimes they behave naturally, as "themselves", while confessing that sometimes they "put on an act". The presumption is that there is an approved "normal" level of behavior very difficult to define which is neither too expressive nor too inexpressive. Behavior can be described as "theatrical" only by those who know what drama is [...]. Behavior is not therefore theatrical because it is of a certain kind but because the observer recognizes certain patterns (12).

The approved "normal" level of behavior can vary from one society to another. Theatricality itself is thus determined by a particular viewpoint, a culturally and socially determined mode of perception, so that misinterpretations may arise when people adhere to certain social norms of which people in another society may be unaware:

People inhabit many social worlds, each of them is a construct, arising from a common perspective held by the members of that world. The behavior that takes place in any of these worlds can appear theatrical to those observers who are not participants or to those newcomers who are just learning the rules. They are acutely aware of the element of composition in the management of sequences of action, which the participants may feel to be spontaneous (13).

Burns continues, claiming that

the line drawn between the two kinds of behavior, theatrical and untheatrical, depends on the selectivity of moral vision which is conditioned by the process of socialization in a particular social milieu, at a particular time. It is not simply a matter of degrees of demonstrativeness. The controlled behavior of a group of upper-class English people at a formal function can appear to observers just as theatrical as the demonstrative behavior of an Italian family greeting each other with kissing and hand-shaking (20).

So, in every culture, there seems to be a generative grammar of behavior as there is of speech (14).

> "Theatricality" in ordinary life consists in the resort to this special grammar of composed behavior; it is when we suspect that behavior is being composed according to this grammar of rhetorical and authenticating conventions that we regard it as theatrical (33).

In terms of *bella figura*, Italians might simply be composing their behavior in a more self-conscious and explicit way than members of other societies, especially the so-called sincerity cultures.

Burns concludes that:

> The issue here, it seems to me, is the question not so much of some ontological difference between "theater" and "real life", being "on" or being "relaxed", but the degree to which composition is conscious or unconscious, important or unimportant, recognizably present or invisible—and, most important of all, socially defined as "normal" or "deviant" (38).

Differences in these social definitions may have their roots in what Burns calls the "concurrent war between puritanism and the stage" (36):

> The importance and nature of the conventions on which theatrical performance rests is easily overlooked, all the more easily because these conventions are for the most part implicit. Conventions are learned in and

through the performance. Yet drama has emerged in both Eastern and Western countries from religious ritual and the performance of religious ritual depends, by contrast, on rules or prescriptions that regulate the movements, actions, gestures, and speech of those involved (23).

Burke seems to agree and writes of a "repudiation of ritual" arising from the Reformation, defining ritual as "a form of communication by action which is public, stereotyped, and symbolic" (225). "The Reformation was, among other things, a great debate, unparalleled in scale and intensity, about the meaning of ritual, its functions, and its proper forms" (226). Ritual seemed empty to reformers, they "denounced traditional Catholic rituals not only as spiritually inefficacious but as harmful, as a means of mystification" (228 f.). The Protestant view that "A true Church keeps simplicity of ceremonies" (232) corresponds with members of "sincerity cultures" accusing Italians of falseness when performing *bella figura*.

In Italian culture, morals and manners are woven together in a way that outsiders do not always fully understand. There is a very specific and complex moral significance of public appearances that Del Negro calls "bodily divination" (66), indicating that Italians frequently seek to gain insights into the inner, moral character of others by inspecting their public performances.

> Bodily displays are seen as an indicator of moral character, and [...] good performance is interpreted as a sign of integrity while bad performance is seen as an indicator of dishonesty or disrespect for the community. In a place where aesthetic display is held in high regard and tied to broader cultural values, artistic accountability becomes a larger sign of moral accountability (61 f.).

This way, artistic power can be converted into social power (62).

"A pleasing countenance not only reveals an affable personality but an interior goodness that transcends manners" (138).

Interestingly, in Italian the word *bello* has a very strong moral significance and is used in contexts in which in English "good" would be the term of choice. For example, *essere una bella persona* ("to be a beautiful person") is a huge compliment, while calling a newborn baby *simpatico* instead of *bellissimo* can seriously damage your relationship to the baby's parents.

In a nutshell, *bella figura* is a public display of appropriate behavior, a general principle of etiquette and taste for all spheres of social life in Italy. Its main aspect is sensitivity to social appropriateness: being generous, polite, respectful, *disinvolto*, well-groomed, meeting or even exceeding expectations and "going the extra mile", while at the same time avoiding arrogance, exaggeration, affectation, falseness and egotistical behavior.

While the Italians themselves are rarely able to explain its cultural significance, they use expressions from the *figura*-family on an everyday basis.

The concept's standards vary from situation to situation, always depending on the respective audience and circumstances, and have changed over the years. Silverman (106), writing about a similar concept, confirms that

> in actual use, different qualities are significant in different situations. In fact, the range covered by the concept and the flexibility of its definition may be the key to its adaptability and its persistence. If certain qualities arise out of earlier conditions [...], they can drop out in favor of other qualities appropriate to later periods (106).

Bella figura is very much what Silverman calls a "fluid ideology" (8).

I HOPE TO HAVE EXPLAINED why it is that to accuse Italians of insincerity when they are performing *bella figura* is to do them wrong. Inauthenticity and insincerity are regarded as morally reprehensible no matter whether you find yourself in the northern or southern hemisphere. One of the few real cultural differences may therefore lie in the degree of social acceptance of composed public performances.

There is certainly more than one kind of *bella figura* behavior. In analogy to what Erving Goffman called an "honest performance", there may be as many forms of more or less honest and sincere *figura* performances as there are Italians. Also, there may well be regional differences between northern and southern Italy. Most of the time, Italians will perform without even realizing it, at other times, actions will be more carefully planned and executed in order to make *gran bella figura*. The "true" *bella figura*, the one that comes from within and earns the most respect, however, is not at all "put on", but requires working hard on improving yourself and constantly showing excellence at whatever you are doing. This is impossible to fake—and it is why Italians do not see any disconnect between sincerity and *bella figura*.

References

Barzini, Luigi. *The Italians: A Full-Length Portrait Featuring Their Manners and Morals*. New York: Atheneum, 1964

Burke, Peter. *The Historical Anthropology of Early Modern Italy: Essays on Perception and Communication*. Cambridge: Cambridge University Press, 1987.

Burns, Elizabeth. *Theatricality: A Study of Convention in the Theatre and in Social Life*. London: Longman, 1972.

Castiglione, Baldassare. *The Book of the Courtier* [*Il libro del cortegiano*]. Transl. Sir Thomas Hoby, 1561. London / New York: Dent / Dutton, 1959.

Del Negro, Giovanna. *The Passeggiata and Popular Culture in an Italian Town: Folklore and the Performance of Modernity*. Montreal: McGill-Queen's University Press, 2004.

Goffman, Erving. *The Presentation of Self in Everyday Life.* New York: Doubleday, 1959.

Goffman, Erving. *Encounters: Two Studies in the Sociology of Interaction.* Indianapolis, IN: Bobbs-Merrill, 1961.

MacClintock, Lander. *The Contemporary Drama of Italy.* Boston: Little, Brown, 1920.

Nardini, Gloria. *Che bella figura!: The Power of Performance in an Italian Ladies' Club in Chicago.* Albany, NY: State University of New York Press, 1999.

Peristiany, J. G. (Ed.). *Honor and Shame: The Values of Mediterranean Society.* Chicago: University of Chicago Press, 1966.

Pitkin, Donald S. "Italian Urbanscape: Intersection of Private and Public." In: *The Cultural Meaning of Urban Space.* Ed. Robert Rotenberg / Gary McDonogh. Westport, CT: Greenwood, 1993, 95-102.

Silverman, Sydel. *Three Bells of Civilization: The Life of an Italian Hill Town.* New York: Columbia University Press, 1975.

Trilling, Lionel. *Sincerity and Authenticity.* London: Oxford University Press, 1972.

MY CZECH REPUBLIC: A USER'S GUIDE TO THE CZECHS

CZECH AUTO- AND HETEROSTEREOTYPING AND AUTO- AND HETEROSTEREOTYPING OF THE CZECHS

BY BEATRIX KRESS

IN A LIST of the most popular Czech proverbs at the end of the twentieth century you will find thirteen different sayings about—the Czechs themselves (Schindler / Bittnerová 1997, 187). That might already indicate a certain tendency among the Czechs to contemplate, to focus attention on, the folk character of their nation, something which can easily be explained by the difficult nation-building process that the Czechs went through during the nineteenth and the first half of the twentieth century, always distinguished from and often in opposition to German culture and the German nation. No wonder that we also find a whole bundle of Czech sayings about the German national character too, or contrasting the Czechs and the Germans. Although it is quite clear that proverbs do not necessarily have to contain "a kernel of truth" (quite often, a proverb can be found that expresses a diametrically opposing point of view, see Schindler 1993, 71), and although from a historical perspective it is not always clear what can be seen as Czech and what as German, proverbs are witnesses to how a ethnic community views itself and its direct neighbor.

The German-Czech relationship is not (and never has been) particularly good. Above and beyond very obviously aggressive sayings like "A good German is a dead German" ("Dobrý němec, mrtvý němec"), there are many that refer to the bad relationship between Czechs and Germans, or the ill intentions of the Germans towards the Czech people: "The German people do nothing for the benefit of the Slavic people" ("Německé plémě se slovanským nic dobrého neobmyšlí"); "He is a German, do not believe him" ("Je Němec, nevěř); "A ploughman will sooner become a prince than a German keep faith with a Czech" ("Spíše oráč dobrým knížetem bude, nežli Němec s Čechy věrně zbude"); and so on. Some of them concentrate on the "feminine charms" of German women, implying that there is no chance of intermarriage and thereby of reconciliation: "A German woman for the stable, a Czech one for the kitchen and a French one for the bed" ("Do chléva Němkyně, Česká do kuchyně, Francouzka do lože (nejlépe se hodí)") or "Better a warm beer than a cold German woman" ("Lepší teplé pivo než studená Němka").

These rather unfavorable descriptions of the German neighbor can and perhaps even *ought* to be seen as part of the struggle for cultural identity. Since the Czechs were a numerically insignificant and stateless people, they were not only in danger of losing their language but also their ethnic identity, before in the Czech National Revival of the nineteenth century well-educated Czechs started to fight Germanization. In fact, many of the proverbs simply point out the difference between Czechs and Germans in language and in identity: "The Czech gets soaked to the skin, the German *durch um durch*" ("through and through") ("Čech promokne na kůži, Němec *durch um durch*"), or "We are we and the Germans are Germans" ("My jsme my, a Němci jsú Němci").

Whereas the Germans appear unfaithful, cold and aggressive—"Wherever a German soldier sets his foot, no grass will grow for seven years" ("Kam německý voják šlápne, tam neroste tráva sedm let")—the Czechs are all in all much more agreeable chaps. For instance, they are very musical, as demonstrated by a proverb that has somehow made its way into German too: "Every Czech is a musician" ("Co Čech, to muzikant"), which reappears in corrupted form as the title of a popular German song, "Music comes from Bohemia". The Czechs are also curious and eager for knowledge ("Co Čech, to výzkumník", "Every Czech is an explorer"). Germans may be unreliable, but the Czechs have always known what belongs to them and what doesn't: "Praví arciotec Čech: Co není tvého, toho nech" ("As our ancestors already said: What doesn't belong to you—keep your hands off it"). While German ways are rather ridiculous— "Na smích lidem všem, po způsobu německém" ("The German disposition is laughed at by everybody")—a Czech knows what he wants: "Čech má hlavu svou, a to neustupnou" ("The Czech has a mind of his own, and he never deviates from that").

Proverbs bear obvious witness to the difficult relationship between the Germans and the Czechs, and document the difficult nation-building process of the latter. But many of these traditional sayings also reveal *autostereotypes* (self-images), and express some of the basic characteristics of Czech culture.

It is an often cited statistic—whether it is true or not—that the Czechs are Europe's champion beer-drinkers (some would even say, the world champions). And so there are no fewer than seventeen proverbs dealing with beer in the list of the most popular Czech sayings (Schindler / Bittnerová, 228).

The trust in beer, as we may put it, is perfectly represented by the proverb "Kde se pivo vaří, tam se dobře daří" ("Where beer is brewed, all is well"). All the other sayings deal with the benefits of beer for your health and your spirits and that it is simply the duty of a Czech man to have his regular glass of beer: "Řeč se mluví, a pivo se pije" ("Language is there to be spoken, and beer is there to be drunk"), or "Očima piva nevypiješ" ("It isn't with your *eyes* that you drink up your beer").

Beer is something that plays a major role in Czech culture— which might suggest a strong link between Germans and Czechs. As evidence of this, there is a very special lexical item both in Czech and in the colloquial language of Southern Germany and

Austria that describes a phenomenon relating to beer-drinking culture: the words *nedopitek* (Czech) and *Noagerl* (German) could be translated into English as "remains", but they are closely associated with beer and the fact that it is out of the question to drink up your beer to the last gulp. You only prove yourself a total fool if you swallow the stale dregs in your glass. Whereas the Czech word refers to that even in its literal meaning (the "no drink up"), the German word is a dialectal variation of the word *Neige* ("remains"), and the prohibition in question is cultural knowledge, as shown by a short paragraph in the *Süddeutsche Zeitung* about Dos and Don'ts at the *Oktoberfest*:

Drink up the *Noagerl*

Beer is expensive at the *Oktoberfest*: you have to fork out 8.90 Euros for one liter in 2010. Despite that fact, the inhabitant of Munich leaves about 10 per cent of the content in his glass and prefers to order a new liter. This is not because there are only bigshots at the *Oktoberfest*. It is tradition. The real locals simply don't drink the *Noagerl*—the last gulp of beer. It is too stale and warm. So never drink up your beer to the last drop—and don't complain when the waitress takes your glass away even though it isn't quite empty: she has your best interests at heart (translated from "Verpönt und verboten—inoffizielle Wiesngesetze", webpage).

What we can see from this tradition is that beer not only plays a major role in Czech culture, but that it is not just something that you consume in order to get drunk (in which case you would likely drink as much of it as possible, to the last drop), but a delicacy. Further evidence that this is something rather special is provided by the *lonely planet* city guide to Prague. Although the authors (in the context of a Prague pub) speak of "the international language of booze" (Baker / Wilson 2009,

187), they also consider it necessary to provide their readers with a chapter on "pub etiquette". There they contrast drinking in Britain with drinking in "Bohemia":

> The waiter will keep track of your order by marking a slip of paper that stays on your table; whatever you do, don't write on it or lose it (you'll have to pay a fine if you do). As soon as the level of beer in your glass falls within an inch of the bottom, the eagle-eyed waiter will be on his/her way with another. But never, as people often do in Britain, pour the dregs of the old glass into the new—this is considered to be deeply uncivilized behavior (177).

The Czech writer and diplomat Jiří Gruša has published a "user's guide to the Czech Republic". It first appeared in German in 1999, but was then translated into Czech and published in Prague in 2001. Gruša also describes the distinctiveness of Czech beer culture, and even goes so far as to relate it to the sacral sphere. He writes that although the word *hospoda* is just the Czech word for a pub it can easily be associated with *Hospodin*, the Czech expression for Lord God. He goes on:

> *Hospoda* contains something sacred in itself. It might be the normal word for pub in Czech, but it somehow evokes *Hospodina*, ruler of the whole world, master of life and death in their entireness. This linguistic relation indicates in a way that the Czechs expect something divine from a pub (48).

Although we have tried to show that there are certain similarities between the Czech and German cultures of drinking, Gruša claims in his description and interpretation of the Czech pub traditions that there are differences. Surprisingly, he sees German culture as rather collectivistic—in contradiction to Hofstede's identification of Germany as an individualistic country, more so than the Czech Republic (see Hofstede / Hofstede 2005, 78)—whereas the Czechs are depicted as individualists in their pub culture. Gruša supports that argument by pointing out the absence of any word like *Stammtisch*, "regulars' table", in the Czech language, and by the fact that the Czech borrowing *štamgast*, from the German word *Stammgast*, "regular (guest)", has a rather negative connotation (49). He is amused by the German word *Bierhalle* ("beer hall"), an institution he associates with the very German activity of *Schunkeln* ("to rock to and fro together"), a tradition that seems rather absurd to him and to Czechs in general (and not only to them).

He describes the Czechs as individualistic beer drinkers:

> The normal Czech is not collectivistic. Drinking together? Yes, sure, but everybody somehow for himself. The jug doesn't circulate within the group. And singing in unison? Maybe, but probably only along with an instrument. And especially: when do I have my solo?! (49)

The importance of beer and of a distinctive pub culture ties in with a well-known auto- and heterostereotype of the Czechs, but the emphasis on the individualism of the Czech people is less common. However, among the whole batch of auto- and heterostereotypes closely linked to the complex of *hospoda* and *pivo*—pub and beer—(rich and heavy food, Schweikian humour *etc.*) there is an autostereotype that might support the idea of an individualistic self-perception: it is the character of the *pábitel*, a person well known in Czech literature. The word *babbler* is almost too weak to describe the character of the *pábitel*, because, even though the amount of talking plays a certain role (his motto is not *cogito ergo sum*, but "I speak, therefore I am", 52), it is actually much more than that. Although the Czech writer Bohumil Hrabal introduced the term into the Czech language with his collection of short stories *Pábitelé* (1964) and, with his Uncle Pepin, gave the phenomenon a literary embodiment, it had already long been present in Czech literature. The good soldier Schweik already knew the art of talking the world into the shape that suited him best. The *pábitel* talks not only for the sake of talking, it is also a matter of making the world a better place by not always keeping strictly to the truth. It is a highly egoistic activity: there is no dialog in the Czech pub, nobody listens to the monolog of his companion, and nobody has to listen to *your* stream of words. The only purpose is to cross the border between reality and fantasy, a task in which a certain amount of beer might be helpful. So what you can observe in the pubs of Prague and all over Bohemia is the realization of the Czech proverb already cited: "Řeč se mluví, a pivo se pije" ("Language is there to be spoken, and beer is there to be drunk").

References

"Verpönt und verboten—inoffizielle Wiesngesetze." In: *sued-deutsche.de.* Website, <no longer online>

Baker, Mark / Wilson, Neil. *Prague City Guide*. London: lonely planet publications, 2009.

Bittnerová, Dana / Schindler, Franz. *Česká přísloví: Soudobý stav konce 20. století*. Prague: Karolinum, 1997.

Gruša, Jiří. *Česko—návod k použití*. Czech edition of the original 1999 publication in German. Prague: Barrister & Principal, 2009.

Hofstede, Geert / Hofstede, Gert Jan. *Cultures and Organizations: Software of the Mind* (1991). Second edition. New York: McGraw-Hill, 2005.

Hrabal, Bohumil. *Pábitelé* (1964). Prague: Mladá fronta, 2006.

Schindler, Franz. *Das Sprichwort im heutigen Tschechischen: Empirische Untersuchung und semantische Beschreibung*. Munich: Kubon & Sagner, 1993.

The translations from Czech and German are by the author.

GREAT EXPECTATIONS

BY CHRISTOPH WERNER

EAST GERMANY, Communist Germany, the German Democratic Republic, the Soviet Occupation Zone, the Eastern Zone or simply "the Zone"—were there even more names for the country which left its imprint on most of my life? Oh yes. Among ourselves we often called it "the greatest GDR in the world". The then (West German) Federal Chancellor Kurt-Georg Kiesinger—having fully recovered from his exhausting job in the Nazi foreign ministry's radio propaganda department, where he was responsible for that ministry's connection with Goebbels' propaganda ministry—tried to avoid any reference to that country by name and once called it *das Gebilde*, which in the context of the time could be translated as "that strange formation".

And verily, a strange formation it was: one which could be hated and loved at the same time. We used to ask each other the following question—in the presence of members of the Communist state party, the SED: In future history books, what will the German Democratic Republic be remembered as? Answer: It will be remembered as a cantankerous, tiny little land on the western frontier of China.

But still—what a country it was. Many poor working-class families sent their children to grammar school and university on scholarships. Health services and most pills were for free (and prescribed so lavishly that checks near surgeries and pharmacies revealed that people often disposed of the medicine in litter bins). More than ninety per cent of the women went out to work and thus gained unheard of status in the family and in society (up to a certain level). Of course they had to take their children to the crèches first, sometimes at 5.30 in the morning, and living in the "chemistry triangle" formed by the cities of Halle, Leipzig and Bitterfeld meant joining your peers in the "bronchitis orchestra". Athletes won Olympic medals galore—strange to say, at the expense of physical education at school. People paid ridiculously low rents—and thus most buildings were in bad repair. Bread was so cheap—subsidized by the state—that clever people fed it to their hens and then sold the eggs to the retail trade. They got a higher price—subsidized by the state—for the eggs than it cost to produce them or even to buy them. So, soon they used a short-cut: they bought eggs in one shop and sold them in another for a higher price, pretending that they (the eggs) were the results of their hens' efforts. This was great fun—for some. The majority paid dearly for this kind of economy, and the state was heavily indebted.

Well, life could indeed be great fun. Take cars. You ordered a car. The choice would cause you neither headache nor heartache, since there were only two models to choose from: the Trabant and the Wartburg. Forgive me: there was also the Skoda from Czechoslovakia, if you had the money. And if you had well-to-do relations in West Germany, generally regarded as the class enemy (West Germany, not your relatives), they could give their hard currency to a state-operated organization by the strange name of Genex, which then gave you a car, first of Eastern make, later also of Western.

If you didn't have any such generous friends or relations in the West (and most people didn't), you had to wait for between twelve and fifteen years before it was your turn. Now people were not stupid. As soon as the children turned eighteen, they were entitled to order a car. And, of course, grandparents and relatives who had never thought of buying or even driving a car could order one. As a result, provided you had a little patience, you could have a new car every few years. And, oh wonder, nearly everybody who wanted a car had a car. Another miracle: usually you could sell your used car for at least the amount of money that you needed to buy a new one.

On the spiritual side, there was a great freedom of opinion in my country. You had the freedom to speak your mind as freely and loudly as you wished! Provided that it didn't differ in any way from the opinion of the dominant party, the SED. Some fools took their constitutional right of freedom of opinion *literally* instead of *dialectically*, and ended up in Hohenschönhausen, a very safe remand prison of the Ministry of Truth—excuse me, Ministry of State Security—where you could be held for two years without being allowed contact to a lawyer. This helped plenty of people to get back on the path of righteousness. Quite a number shortened their stay by promising to help the Ministry in its endeavors to gather as much information as possible about its charges, *i.e.*, the population of the country.

But here as in many other cases the class enemy in West Germany helped generously. It bought the prisoner, let us say for DM 30,000, and set him or her free in West Germany. So they got their freedom, and the GDR got hard currency, with which it could then buy goods in West Berlin that were urgently needed in Wandlitz, where the members of the Politbureau— the high command of the country—lived behind barbed wire and well protected by the comrades of the State Security Police.

As indicated, if you kept mum you could live well. Take your humble author, who kept mum enough to be allowed to study English and German at the Martin-Luther-University in Halle-Wittenberg from 1957 to 1962. No chance of going to England to improve my English, though. Not even after I had made love to a member (female) of the Communist Party of Great Britain who visited the GDR to tell people there about the British Campaign for Nuclear Disarmament and sing the relevant songs (rather shrilly, I have to say). She invited me to London—a dream of cosmic proportions for a student of English in East Germany— on behalf of her London-based Communist Party branch. But the authorities refused to grant me a visa, the reason being that, as the GDR had no diplomatic relations with the UK at that time, they could not let me go unprotected to an imperialist country! So we had to content ourselves in our institute with a lonely Communist from Liverpool, who had chosen to spend the rest of his life in paradise. But as he was a good teacher and his English was more or less understandable, and as we had an excellent phonetic training, we made do.

To make do, that is what generally helped people to survive and even enjoy life within well-defined limits. For many, East Germany could be an idyll, though in truth a frightful one. The dictatorship appeared in the garb of fatherly love. It rewarded the well-behaved and punished the naughty, not to destroy them, though, but to make them better. If you regretted your outrage you could hope for a mitigation of punishment. The main road to this kind of redemption was self-criticism.

Even those who secretly hated the system and refused to play an active role could find a small corner of harmony with like-minded spirits, who often gathered under the protection of the local church. Nationwide the upper echelons of the clergy had made their peace with the regime. A sizable number served the secret police as informants. But parish priests opened their churches on Mondays for all who wanted to take part in what came to be called "peace prayers". The secret police sent their people to these prayers to learn who had taken part and what had been said. Your author once heard the minister of a church in the city of Halle greet those present with the words "I am particularly glad to welcome those among you who came here not so much to pray but to listen and to observe. Let us include them and their families in our prayers." With this he looked at some people sitting at the back for so long that everybody turned their heads to look at them, too. And, hard as it may be to believe, some of them even blushed.

But most people in East Germany had made a kind of deal with the regime, persuading themselves that they didn't really participate in the prevailing injustice but only pretended to. They were able to develop a very efficient doublethink. At work they talked the way official propaganda demanded, but privately they longed for the sort of life that was shown on West German television.

Understandably, this difficult tight-rope walk didn't leave people undamaged. Drinking was widespread, and the GDR belonged to the countries with the highest per capita consumption of alcohol. People sought to compensate for their frustration by seeking as many sexual encounters as possible, men and women alike. And if this was not possible for some, they at least told each other dirty and, even more often, political jokes. The rate of suicide was high and so was the rate of mental illness.

Does all this sound contradictory, inconsistent? If so, it sounds right, because the system *was* contradictory, inconsistent and, to a high degree, openly ridiculous. But it was dangerous, even lethal, for those who decided that they had to resist, to dissent, to speak up.

That was a glimpse of the background against which my family and I applied for emigration to West Germany. It was only after my wife had lost her job and after repeated interrogations by the secret police that we were finally granted permission to leave the country.

We crossed the frontier six weeks before the Berlin Wall came down, after which you could travel freely. Still, we were happy enough not to feel ridiculous.

Hanover in Lower Saxony was where my brother lived. He had left East Germany in 1953, at the tender age of fourteen, at a time when the frontier between East and West Berlin was still open. You simply got on the municipal railway and went west. He put us up, and we had the chance of unhurriedly getting used to life in the free world.

I was fifty years old when we left East Germany and came to the west.

SUDDENLY, MONEY-PROCURING EGGS, cars, mental illness, casual sexual encounters, and so on all lost their importance and other things came to the foreground. The gift of doublethink that I mentioned above was now applied to the contradictions of a *democratic* society, which was less harmful to one's health.

As we had always watched West German television and talked to our relatives who had come to visit us in East Germany, there were many things that did not surprise us, but others did.

In the allegedly money-determined, materialistically-minded cold capitalist world we met mainly friendly people—and that says a lot, seeing that we were in Lower Saxony. Even the police, the local authorities, people in the labor exchange, the housing office and the town hall were helpful.

The first shock I had was when I tried to buy some meat, or was it sausage, for the family. The display of meat products in the supermarket appeared to me so large, the choice so exaggerated, even superfluous, almost sinful, that I had to break off my shopping and hurry home because I feared I was going to be sick. While I got used to many other things fairly quickly, it took me longest to come to terms with the extravagance, the squandering, with respect to food.

I was lucky enough to get a job at a small university near Hanover very soon as a lecturer in English. Though I was just filling in for a colleague who had gone to America on paternity leave for two years, I struck a bonanza. Firstly, because I earned what I regarded at that time as a lot of money, and secondly, because I underwent a kind of forced socialization in a very short time which would otherwise (probably) have taken many years.

There is a myth concerning the differing work ethics in East and West Germany before the reunification of the country. The West Germans generally believed that the East Germans were a lazy lot who after 1989 had to be taught what it was like to work hard. Now, at my new place of work I was surprised to find that the work load you took upon yourself was defined by you yourself. If you wanted to take it easy, workwise, you could. Nobody cared, except maybe the students. But since they had to pass examinations and therefore didn't want to alienate their examiners, *i.e.*, their lecturers, they rarely complained.

In a comparable position in East Germany I had had to teach twenty forty-five minute periods a week and spend at least another twenty hours doing administration and research. In my new academic institution it was twelve hours teaching and not much else (if you so decided). Some members of staff, some of them quite senior, managed to come to work only two and a half days per week. The rest could be whiled away at home, with some people earning money on the side by doing translations or writing reports for industrial enterprises. To be fair, though, the majority of the staff worked their share, some of them even more than that, and so helped to keep the university going.

What topped it all was what I later learned during a summer term spent at another German university. The paternity leave colleague had come back from America and I had to find a new job. I had heard on the grapevine that at the University of X somebody in the field of English teacher training wanted to take a year's sabbatical and so they needed a temporary lecturer. As I had never before worked in this area, training future English teachers, my expertise was—to say the least—rudimentary. But to my lasting amazement both the students and I myself survived. This must have had something to do with that peculiarity of work in academia, where you so often disguise your lack of knowledge by euphonious and often mysterious words or word-combinations that are difficult to understand and therefore difficult to contradict.

In my academic life in the east this had not been so, probably because Marxist-Leninist vocabulary was expected to be stringent, unambiguous, and not in the least fanciful.

But this was not the surprising new discovery that I referred to earlier. This stupendous item was the piece of advice that I got from a well-meaning comrade-in-arms when I arranged my timetable for the term. Why didn't I put four hours of class (of my weekly twelve) on Friday afternoon, he queried, eyebrows raised? I said that in my experience students didn't appreciate seminars on Friday afternoons and thus the classes might have to be cancelled. He looked me straight in the eye for quite some time, until I—clumsy beast from the East—understood. No further word was required, and my working week for that term thereafter consisted of eight teaching periods a week. Henceforth I called this the "Friday method".

That same colleague had organized his own timetable in an enviably ingenious way, which showed the creativity that is possible in a capitalist free-enterprise society as compared to the unproductive and inefficient command society I had escaped from. The colleague, who as a senior lecturer had to teach only eight hours of seminars a week, had managed to put all his teaching on one day, Monday, after reducing it by means of the Friday method to six hours. The rest of the time he spent in his privately-run esoteric marriage counseling office just opposite the main building of the university. This helped him to put aside a nice little bundle, which he needed, however, as he had been divorced a few times and had to take financial care of his former wives and his children. Also, through his marriage counseling he had found himself a girlfriend—and she happened to be someone who was not to be enjoyed cheaply.

After the term was over I went back to my small university in Lower Saxony, where in the meantime a professorship in English language teaching had been put on the market. Now it is often so in Germany that it takes years to find a suitable professor. And it did. So— happy me could fill in for four years.

What I have tried to do, dear reader, is to tell you what I did before I went into early retirement and could start pondering what it meant to have experienced two such different cultures as East and West Germany before they fused into one.

Allow me to close by telling you about a dream that I had, one which gave me the fright of my life.

You may remember how in August 1991 Communist hardliners in the Soviet Union attempted a *coup d'état* against President Mikhail Gorbachev.

I watched television on the second day of the putsch, when Gorbachev was still confined to his Foros dacha on the Crimea. I went to bed and had this dream: the hardliners had won, and led the crumbling Soviet Union back into the Ice Age of Stalinist Communism. Newly united Germany was to be split up again and East Germany to be returned to the Soviet Union. All former East Germans now living in the West were to be repatriated (if need be by force) to East Germany. The police (West German) came to our house and marched my family and me to the station in Hanover where the train to East Berlin was waiting.

Just as we were on the point of being bundled onto the train, I woke up, my heart beating wildly. I realized where I was, calmed down and felt in a moment of unbelievable happiness that, after all, my great expectations had been fulfilled.

CHILI PEPPER MEETS SAUERKRAUT

MEXICANS AND GERMANS—TWO CONTRASTING IDENTITIES
BY MARÍA ELENA CAMACHO-MOHR

GERMANS ARE TALL, have blond hair and live on sausage and sauerkraut. They drink lots of beer, and wear the traditional Bavarian *Lederhosen*, those short leather pants reaching just to the knee, supported with straps over the shoulders. Germans are tidy and punctual and they work hard and effectively. They are arrogant and pedantic. Germans lack humor and flexibility.

Mexicans like to wear huge sombreros. They drink tequila, with salt and a lime wedge, and are constantly eating tacos and nachos with a big portion of chili peppers. They are lazy, unpunctual and always prefer "siesta" and "fiesta". Their favorite word is *"mañana"*, because nothing is so important that it has to be done today—you always can do it tomorrow.

There are many stereotypes of these two peoples. Although some of them are ridiculous, it is easy to be hoodwinked by them. I remember a story I read in a book by Christian Graf von Krockow (1999). It's about an Englishman traveling through France who was anxious to get to know everything about the country and its culture. As he stopped by a street café in Calais, his first destination in France, he was served by a waiter with red hair. So he immediately wrote down in his note-book: "In France the waiters have red hair" (65, my translation).

But are some of the stereotypes perhaps true to some degree? Surely it always depends on your own experience, whether you consider these stereotypes and prejudices true or false. I am a Mexican girl. Even before I came to Germany, I had already had my own experience of German people, which—for the first time—made me change my opinion about them and how they are.

Germans are likable, friendly and funny. They are extroverted, eloquent and very active, they like to dance, to have crazy parties and new adventures. Germans are always curious and they have an open mind about new things and people. I got to know a lot of Germans. And I knew those German people very well. Well, that's what I thought, at least! Then I came to Germany. And I was wrong. The characteristics of the Germans that I now met were not the complete opposite of those mentioned above, but they were different. Yes, they were quite different from the way they had been in the place where I first got to know them, in the holiday paradise of Playa del Carmen, in the Mexican Caribbean, where I had been living for a while. So I realized how naïve I had been in Playa del Carmen, just like the Englishman in France. And therefore I had to change my opinion about the Germans once again.

This article is an opportunity for me to write about some of the experiences that Mexican people have in Germany, with the Germans and their culture, and compare this with the Mexican way of life. It might even reveal what the Germans are really like. In some cases I have compared my experiences with the experience of Mexican culture that Germans have in Mexico. Interviewing as I did Mexicans who live in the north of Germany, their experiences—like mine—might be different from those of a Mexican who lives, for example, in the west of Germany near Cologne, where Carnival is called the "fifth season of the year" and a huge party is celebrated over several weeks, or in the east, where the people of East Germany (the German Democratic Republic, 1949-1990) lived somewhat different lives for more than forty years. For when you travel through Germany you notice that German people can be significantly different from one area to the next.

When Mexicans come to Germany, they often experience a kind of culture shock. This is what happened to me when I noticed that the Germans were not as friendly and extroverted as I had known them in Mexico—as tourists. My first encounters with Germans in their own country were rather cold meetings, and they didn't seem to be very interested in me as a person. It was then that I realized that not a single German—apart from my husband and his friends—had really been waiting for me to arrive or automatically wanted to be my friend. I felt very lonely and went through a hard time. In Mexico, it's easier to find someone to have a good time with, because Mexicans are generally more approachable and open than Germans. But when you have finally made a German friend, which might take a long time, you'll have them forever. The friendships seem to be deeper than in Mexico. A lot of Mexicans here in Germany have also had this experience.

Another shock was the language. German is so hard to learn! At first, you can't follow a conversation very well, because you are always waiting for the verb in the sentence, since only when you have heard it can you understand the sense of what the speaker was saying. Sometimes it's a long wait, if the main part of the verb (or even the whole verb) is, as so often happens in German, at the end of the sentence: "He has a woman with six children, two cats, a dog and an incredible number of debts *married*", and that's a word-for-word translation of a fairly *short* sentence! Once I arrived late for a lecture at the university. I sat down and was listening to the lecturer but I couldn't understand what he was talking about. So I asked my neighbor what the lecturer was saying, and he answered in broken German: "I don't know what he wants to tell us, he's already been talking for ten minutes but he hasn't used a verb yet." OK, I'm just kidding, it's an old joke, but this is exactly how you feel when you start to learn German.

After a bit you can follow German conversations and, with

this newly-gained skill, you want to learn more about German culture and understand everything. So some Mexican friends and I went to a German cinema. It was great! We went to one of those huge cinema complexes with about ten screening rooms that you can find in every big town in Germany. It reminded us immediately of the cinema centers in Mexico, and for a moment we felt quite at home. But then we tasted the popcorn. What an awful shock! It was disgusting, sickly sweet. We Mexicans *never, ever* sweeten the popcorn—we eat it with salt or with a spicy sauce, but with sugar? It was nauseating. It felt as if you had bought a vanilla ice and instead of delicious ice-cream you had dipped your tongue into a blob of mayonnaise.

Fine, that's ten years ago, and nowadays a lot of German cinemas offer salted popcorn and even nachos and cheese. So we Mexicans have calmed down a bit in the meantime.

A German restaurant is another place where you might have an odd experience at the beginning of your stay in the country. When I entered a restaurant for the first time, I waited at the entrance for someone to come and show me to a seat. It was a long wait, maybe ten minutes, which felt like an eternity to me. Then, finally, a waiter came and asked whether he could help me, or was I maybe looking for someone? Then it dawned on me that you were expected to find your own table, whereas in Mexico you wait at the entrance for someone to invite you in and guide you to the table he has chosen for you. Most German people prefer this more anonymous way of doing things, and being able to choose a table on their own. It seems that Germans always like to decide independently, and they tell me that they actually get annoyed if they are steered towards a particular seat—they consider that they are being imposed upon rather than offered a service.

It was similar, initially, when I went shopping for groceries. I would be looking for something, but there would be nobody to ask for help apart from a few customers and just one shop assistant at the checkout counter. Once the cashier of a supermarket said, "one moment please, I'll be right back," and went off to help another customer who was looking for a particular article. Meanwhile, other customers joined the queue and people were getting more and more upset due to the long wait. I missed the service in the supermarkets we have in Mexico. In every section there is at least one shop assistant who is ready and pleased to help you. Then at the checkout counter there are employees who will pack your purchases into the complimentary plastic bags. Now that's what I call good service!

Another thing we Mexicans need a lot of time to get used to is the highly-developed culture of environmental protection in Germany. For example, you are expected to collect and sort paper, packaging, glass, and organic waste. Separately, and at regular intervals, each of these different types of trash will be picked up by the appropriate garbage truck in front of your house. Even batteries have to be collected and taken to a special collection point, for example in your supermarket. Germans are probably the world champions in recycling. In Mexico, environmental protection is still in its infancy. So it isn't easy for us Mexicans to get used to doing it the German way, even after some years in Germany.

"Turn off the light, you are wasting electricity." "You are not in the kitchen, so why have you left the radio on?" "Let's save energy and *walk* into town!" We get used to hearing things like this from our German partners. And should you disagree—let's say, for instance, because you are simply not in the mood for a 45-minute walk downtown, followed by some promenading up and down when you arrive there, and then another 45-minute walk back home—you're likely to get into a full-blown discussion with them about it. In order to save energy—*my* energy—I tend to cave in right away and agree with my husband on matters like these.

Environmental protection is very important, sure, and probably I've started to think more like a German on this issue. I separate the trash, and I don't buy plastic bags at the supermarket anymore, though this might also have something to do with saving money (I'm thinking about those free plastic bags at the supermarkets in Mexico). I save water by pressing the "reduced flush" button on the toilet, and while, I'm afraid, I still like to take a long, hot shower to relax, at least I now do so with a guilty conscience.

There are so many rules in Germany, and if you don't observe them, some German will soon make you aware of it. Older people especially like to make sure that their fellow citizens keep to the rules. As I once read in a book long ago, "In every German there's a hidden policeman" (Larson 1983, 17). And there's some truth in that. For example, a lot of Mexicans have been rebuked by older Germans for riding a bike on the sidewalk or for jaywalking. Once or twice, when I crossed the street while the light was still red, Germans yelled at me that I was "badly brought up". But I only did this when there was no traffic, and no child anywhere in sight to whom I might be setting a bad example! So where was the sense in waiting around for no reason?

In big cities in Mexico you see a lot of people, even families with children, crossing against the light despite heavy traffic. Or crossing streets where there are no traffic lights instead of using a nearby footbridge. They want to save time, and with this excuse they actually risk their lives—and no one gives a damn about it. This is the other extreme. The drivers don't care about traffic rules, so on Mexican streets you will always find utter chaos, and Germans are terrified of venturing out into this, whether in a car or on foot. They really miss their good old German traffic regulations.

There are rules in German home life, too, and one of them is punctuality. "Dinner is at seven o'clock." That means that if you arrive late, say at twenty past seven, you may have to eat alone, or you'll get a lukewarm meal, because everyone else started eating at exactly seven o'clock. And the host will make his or her displeasure very clear to you. (By the way, Germans usually say "too late" rather than just "late"—as in "Hurry up, we don't want to be too late for the lecture!"—which is semantically dubious but reflects the attitude to punctuality quite well.) No hope here for Mexicans! But as a kind of consolation, younger Germans now seem to be growing out of the punctuality obsession.

Nevertheless even young Germans have a problem in Mexico with the word "*ahorita*", which can mean "a minute ago", "right now", "in a minute", or "soon"—and "soon" can mean almost anything, even "in a few hours". When they ask, for example, "when do we leave?" or "what time are we going to meet your friends at the bar?" they get the answer "*ahorita!*" instead of precise information. They might be able to guess the meaning of the word in this context, but they can never be sure. Not even Mexicans know exactly, when they use the word, but they don't mind! However, this uncertainty and imprecision makes Germans nervous, even angry.

And how do you say hello, when you meet people? In Mexico, when you say hello or good bye you kiss each other on the right cheek. In Germany, you give a handshake or a hug, but seldom a kiss. This can be a cause of irritation, if a Mexican wants to kiss a German to say hello. Germans may be a bit startled and step back, because they're not sure what it is that the Mexican wants to do so close to their face! Germans need greater interpersonal distance than Mexicans in order to feel comfortable. It may happen that a German attempts the kiss-greeting, but chooses the wrong side, that is to say the left cheek, so that innocent lips meet each other for an involuntary kiss. That can be very funny, but also embarrassing. And once, when an attractive Mexican girl tried to welcome a German guy with the kiss on the cheek, he misunderstood the situation and gave her a passionate French kiss...

In Germany, people will stick out their hand towards you in greeting, particularly the older generation. And there is a very German way of saying hello or goodbye to a group by rapping on the table that everyone is sitting at, to save having to address people individually. Sometimes I really miss those kisses.

On the other hand, I have observed German teenagers give each other a mouth-to-mouth kiss as a welcome (though not when both of them were men). That's a very warm welcome, in fact to my mind rather *too hot*. It's quite a contrast between the way starchy older people behave—and these German teenagers! And why do they do it? Is it perhaps to distinguish best friends from just good ones? Or do they want to be as different as possible from their parents, even if it means carrying things to extremes? In Mexico the kiss on the mouth is a very intimate matter, reserved only for lovers. Between parents and children, or between friends, we are happy enough with the good old kiss on the right cheek.

Speaking of family, the parent-child relationship in Germany is very different to that in Mexico. In Germany you see a lot of parents explaining almost everything to their kids from the cradle onwards. And always giving reasons why the kids should or shouldn't do something. Education in México is more authoritarian. There the answer to "but why not?" will be "because I say so!"—and that's that.

Very early on, many German parents will speak to their kids about "the birds and the bees". And certainly no later than the onset of puberty, girls in particular will be told the facts of life again—but in greater detail—and taken to a gynecologist by their mothers very soon afterwards. From then on many girls will be allowed to go on the pill to minimize the risk of pregnancy. Some German parents have told me that although they allowed this, it wasn't a free ticket for the girls to have sex, but just a kind of protection "in case". "Be careful, don't have a one night stand! Guys are always on the look-out for a new girl to seduce," says the father to his daughter. "I'm a man, I know how men think." The mother might add, "But if it happens, please make him use a condom," which may displease the father and kick off a disagreement between the parents. Because what the father is probably really thinking is: "I'm gonna kill the goddamn guy who has sex with my daughter!"

German parents know that they can't control their children all the time, and so they arm them with a good knowledge of the facts of life. From about sixteen, many German teenagers will even be allowed to have their boy- or girlfriend "sleep over".

For us Mexicans this is all amazingly progressive. It would be unthinkable in Mexico. There the name of the game is still "no sex before marriage!" and parents won't even talk about it. When you introduce your boy- or girlfriend to your parents, you are already effectively announcing that it's a serious relationship and you can now be as good as considered engaged. So you'd better not introduce him or her to your parents if you are not yet that sure whether it's serious or not.

As a result, a lot of children hide their affairs from their parents, and when they want to sleep together, they go to one of the numerous motels. This is an open secret that the parents know about only too well—after all, they did it themselves when they were young! But even if it's a really serious relationship, you still go to those famous motels with your partner, because "no sex until marriage" includes "don't even *try* to do it at home" and "always sleep in your own bed, and always alone!" Going on vacation or staying somewhere overnight is generally not permitted. The parents argue that that way the children "can't fall into temptation".

In Mexico, having sex before marriage—above all when women do it—still means that the family honor is soiled. And—worse still—should the girl get pregnant, as the saying goes "*se comió la torta antes del recreo*" (best translated as "she ate the cake before the wedding"), the two concerned families will try to organize the wedding in a great hurry, before people notice her big belly. All this is a clear case of double standards: on the one hand, the innocence of the children and the reputation of the family in the eyes of the church and of society, and on the other hand the open secret of the "tell-no-tales motels".

Children in Mexico who are not married yet have to keep on living with their parents, because they have no reason to leave. So it happens that there are "children" who are 25 or 30 years old or even older and still live with their parents. In Germany, if you are still living with your parents at that age people will think that there's something wrong with you ("mommy's darling", *etc.*). Most young Germans prefer to live away from home once they get a job or go to university. It doesn't matter whether you are married or not. Young people in Germany are much more independent than they are in Mexico, which is very enviable. On the other hand, in Mexico family members stay together more, irrespective of age or marital status, whether because of closer family bonds or just tighter finances.

There is also a big difference between Germany and Mexico in how marriage partners behave towards each other. Basically, it's German emancipation versus Mexican machismo. In Germany many husbands will help in the household, cleaning up, putting the kids to bed, cooking, putting the trash out or shopping for groceries, and often both husband and wife will go out to work. Wife and husband generally enjoy equal rights, and in some families it is the "house-husband" who stays at home, does the housework and looks after the kids.

Unthinkable in Mexico! Out of the question. The Mexican husband goes out to work; his wife stays at home and does all the rest. Or even worse, sometimes she'll have to work as well, but that won't change anything at home, where she still has to do everything. A man who stays at home to keep house is not a real man! (That's what the machos think, at least.) Many Mexican women, however, disagree, and rather sympathize with the idea of emancipation. So they appreciate German husbands and admire the way they behave within the marriage.

Last year some Mexican women got the biggest surprise of their lives when they came to Germany to visit their daughters and their German families. They all went out together to a birthday party and at the end of the event everything had to be cleared up. But the Mexican ladies remained seated and kept on drinking and chatting, while their German husbands cleaned up the whole place. The Mexican mothers couldn't believe their eyes! But for the German men it was quite normal—and not totally unselfish either, because it was late and they wanted to go home to bed. Mexican women are used to talking on and on without end, as their German husbands had learned by now, so the men preferred to take the initiative instead of waiting endlessly for their wives and spending all night at the party.

After living in Germany for a few years, we've gotten over most of the culture shocks and used to many aspects of the German way of life, sometimes even to the point that we prefer them, like for example the higher level of safety and the less chaotic traffic in Germany. Now, the culture shocks come when we go back to Mexico—which is a strange feeling.

Looking at German cultural identity as we Mexican expatriates experience it daily, we come to understand the things that matter to Germans and which shape the way they are: having a secure and well-paid job, a beautiful place to live and a nice car, and being able to go on vacation at least once a year. An elementary need is to have a secure future, as in knowing that you will get a good pension and have enough money to be comfortable when you grow old. Germans work very hard for this, with a lot of self-discipline. They need savings, and insurance. Many of them seem to view life as a big struggle, find it difficult to relax, and feel really bad if one of these "essentials" is missing.

Mexicans, in contrast, prefer to live their lives on a day-to-day basis. They don't save much, don't have a lot of insurance, and don't worry too much the future; what matters is spending time with your family, going out with friends or for a meal, and spending your money when you like and on what you like rather than saving it up for the obligatory vacation getaway or for a "rainy day". In other words—just living.

These are the Mexicans and Germans as I know them, which is why I'm rather skeptical about Hofstede's assessment of the Mexicans as being higher "uncertainty avoidance" than the Germans (Hofstede / Hofstede 1991, 168 f.). Not in my experience!

Inevitably, when two cultures encounter each other, they will influence each other, and it's nice to see how Mexican culture has begun to weave its magic in Germany in certain ways. Here are just a couple of examples. Since the Nineties, "*la ola*" has been a regular part of the action in German football stadiums.

This is the famous Mexican wave created by successive groups of spectators briefly standing and raising their arms before they sit down again, all the way around the stadium, cheering for their favorite team or players. It was the 1986 football World Cup in Mexico that inspired this.

Then there is the Mexican "*piñata*", increasingly a feature of German children's birthday parties. This is a brightly-colored decoration made from cardboard, covered with *papier-mâché* and filled with candy, which is hung up somewhere central where everyone can see it. The children open it by pulling its strings all at once or by clubbing it—then there is a shower of candy, and the children rush about, quickly picking the treats up from the floor.

At German parties for adults you can drink tequila, though you need to be careful with this Mexican agave *schnapps* because most of the stuff sold in German supermarkets is really bad, with a sickly taste, and will give you an awful headache the day after. If you want to taste good tequila, it has to be "100 per cent Agave". For this quality, though, you'll need to pay a small fortune in Germany, which is probably why hardly any Germans are familiar with really good tequila.

And, finally, there is Mexican food, which is becoming ever more popular in Germany. This might be connected with the World Fair 2000 in Hanover, where the fiestas at the Mexican pavilion were a great success, but also with the growing number of Germans who spend their holidays in Mexico. So in almost every German town nowadays you'll be able to find Mexican food or at least Tex-Mex.

It may not always be authentic—just adding some kidney beans, sweet corn and chili to the dishes won't on its own make them genuinely Mexican. But there are some interesting new cross-over dishes, like that delicious insider tip "Chili con Sauerkraut". What next? Who knows! *¡Viva la globalización!*

References

Hofstede, Geert / Hofstede, Gert Jan. *Cultures and Organizations: Software of the Mind* (1991). Second edition. New York: McGraw-Hill, 2005.

Krockow, Christian Graf von. *Über die Deutschen*. Munich: List, 1999.

Larson, Bob. *Getting along with the Germans* (1983). Esslingen: Bechtle, 2000.

DRINKS AT THE ADELPHI
AN INTERVIEW WITH T. W. GERAGHTY

EDITOR'S NOTE: The veteran Irish writer, scholar, intercultural commentator, journalist and raconteur T. W. Geraghty (the "Sage of Galway") agreed to submit to the indignities of an interview, which took place (at his request) in the bar at the Adelphi Hotel in Liverpool.

Interviewer. Well, good afternoon, and thank you for agreeing to this meeting. You've seen a lot of the world. Is Liverpool one of your favourite hunting grounds?

Geraghty. You mean, because of the Irish connection? Maybe. Liverpool's been a very lively city, culturally speaking, for hundreds of years now. Fleshed out—if you'll excuse the expression—by the Slave Trade, pumping out cheap Manchester crap to the colonies, then there was the big influx from Ireland because of the Potato Famine, all those sailors from God knows where, massive unemployment—and you do know what unemployment encourages? Petty crime, taxi driving, and sitting around feeling sorry for yourself, for Chrissake, which in some people leads to artistic and literary activity...

Interviewer. Not to mention the Beatles?

Geraghty. Oh, I'd include them under "artistic", God bless them! And two of the lads at least, Lennon and McCartney, with most suspiciously Irish-sounding names. "Harrison" could come from anywhere, I suppose, though I'm told there may have been an Irish family link.

Interviewer. Liverpool probably isn't the worst place to be interviewing someone who has devoted so much of his life to the study of intercultural communication and multicultural situations.

Geraghty. Now that's a pompous way of putting it! I've travelled a lot, to be sure. I've done some lecturing and talking. And I've published a few bits and pieces, though most of it's out of print now.

Interviewer. Republishing things is no problem today, what with books on demand technology and the internet. Aren't you tempted to get some of the stuff republished?

Geraghty. No, the world has moved on. Makes me think of old E. M. Forster, writing his gay novel *Maurice* and then hiding it in his knickers for decades! OK, he circulated it among his more tolerant writer friends, but when he could finally, eventually, publish it without being, you know, publicly tarred and feathered as a degenerate homosexualist deviant, it would have seemed tame and Edwardian, wouldn't it, competing with the likes of *The Naked Lunch* or *Last Exit to Brooklyn*? It wouldn't have worked. Some of what I wrote years ago may have seemed like steaming hot chocolate at the time, but today?

Anyways, there's so much new stuff to be thought about. This is one old dog who doesn't like returning to his vomit.

Interviewer. So you don't want to discuss the past? Places you've been, for instance?

Geraghty. I've been to some great places. Maybe I've even been drawn to places where cultures rub up against each other.

You know, Shanghai, Beirut, Northern Ireland for that matter! There's a lot on the menu in places like that, and I don't mean just food. The crack [Irish, meaning "lively, enjoyable conversation"—*Ed.*] is good. And you know something? We intercultural people are always wittering on about the possible synergy effects when you have cultural diversity. Stating the obvious, I would have thought. But what matters much more is that cultures should *challenge* each other. So that you're not just sitting there all smug in your monocultural bog. Stewing in your orthodoxy. Congratulating yourself that *your* culture gets it right every time. You do *that* for too long, young man, and your cultural balls will drop off! When you have to confront different cultural attitudes, different values, day in, day out, *that's* when you find out what your own beliefs are.

Interviewer. So does that mean that, essentially, you're a multiculturalist?

Geraghty. Jesus, you've not been listening! I said "confront", didn't I? If you really want to know, I'm a Late Enlightenment, Western European universalist who says his daily prayer to Voltaire and happens to think that modern Western civilization is—to date, at least—the peak, the zenith, of centuries of human endeavor. Sorry, now it's me that's being pompous!

Interviewer. When Gandhi was asked what he thought of Western civilization, he said he thought that it would be a good idea.

Geraghty. Clever, that! Of course it didn't stop him turning to Western medicine (rather than traditional Indian ayurvedic medicine) when his own life was in danger.

I'm not denying that we owe a lot to, you know, Indian civilization, or Judaism, or the Arabs in the Middle Ages. And I'm not saying that we can't learn from other cultures. Quite the opposite, in fact. The greatness of our own civilization is that it's such a bastard, mongrel thing, with intellectual genes from all over the bloody place! I *am* saying that we shouldn't sell out what we hold dear—the freedoms and the tolerance and the decencies that our ancestors bought at high cost—because of some wishy-washy multiculturalism, some spineless cultural relativism.

Interviewer. Isn't that a bit of a contradiction? You're talking about tolerance, but at the same time you seem to arguing for an *intolerant* attitude towards other cultures.

Geraghty. Do you really think so? Look—we *have* to listen to each other, and try to understand each other, otherwise we won't learn anything. If you have even a modicum of intelligence, that is the default position.

Interviewer. Do I hear a faint echo of Martin Buber there?

Geraghty. Indeed, *pace* Buber, I've never denied all that stuff about finding your identity in the mirror of the Other, *etc.* We're all globalized, it goes without saying, we're all networked, these days. We *have* to listen to each other. But dialog—that much overused word—isn't some kind of mutual masturbation, it's a search for the truth.

Interviewer. Sorry, I still think you're contradicting yourself. It was you who brought up the idea of tolerance as a Western value. Surely that's what the relativists are after? Acknowledgement of difference leading to mutual *respect*?

Geraghty. If all values are of more or less equal worth, which tends to be the relativist position, why bother with dialog at all? And if they're all equal, or equally right, that's a moral cop-out. You might just as well say that they're all equally wrong, or equally worthless. Tolerance doesn't mean total, uncritical acceptance: "I'll scratch your back, you scratch mine." Liberal relativists in Western cultures are pretty well the only people in the world who take such a view. I'll tell you something—outside their circles, it's not even a stance that's much respected, it's often interpreted as a sign of weakness. Or stupidity. Which perhaps it is! They don't get *their* backs scratched very much, not by the likes of the Taliban.

Buber was a lovely guy, truly, but when there's a wolf behind every second tree, it's time to stop playing Little Red Riding Hood. [*Laughs*] If you catch my drift.

Interviewer. To be honest, I'm not sure that I do. Essentially, though, we need to fight our cultural corner, is that what you're saying?

Geraghty. Yes. If you truly believe something, you'll put up a fight for it. That's what it's always been about. This linking of freedom with individual responsibility is a central theme of our civilization. It runs like a golden thread, from Pericles's Funeral Oration to the Gettysburg Address right down to that inscription at the Korean War Memorial in Washington which says "Freedom Is Not Free". The core values of your culture, ideas that are part of the makeup of your identity—you have to stick up for them, otherwise you'll lose yourself.

Interviewer. And you don't think that's happening anymore in the Western world? Not even with military interventions in Iraq and Afghanistan and so on? Surely the West is being pro-active, aggressive, not reticent!

Geraghty. You know very well what a bugger it was organizing those "coalitions of the willing"! And still is. We left the Tutsis to rot in Rwanda, didn't we? And why was that? Because they didn't have any oil? Because they were black? There's a thought... No, let's not bring race into it! But perhaps: "A quarrel in a far-away country between people of whom we know nothing" [British Prime Minister Neville Chamberlain abandoning the Czechs to Hitler's mercy in 1938—*Ed.*]?

And think how long it took before anyone got properly stuck into it in Yugoslavia, to stop the horrors that were going on there. All those human rights abuses going on in a European country just around the corner—ethnic cleansing, concentration camps, gang rapes, mutilations, massacres—and the Europeans sitting on their hands. No, we're in "wag your tail and roll over and let them tickle your tummy" mode most of the time. At least when we're faced with fanatics and fundamentalists who know exactly what they want and who mean business.

It used to be called "appeasement". To quote a great fellow countryman of mine: "The best lack all conviction, while the worst / Are full of passionate intensity" [W. B. Yeats, *The Second Coming*, 1919—*Ed.*]. And while I'm quoting, let me just say this... Damaged as I am by all those grim years of traditional Irish schooling, I hate to have to agree with the Catholic Big Fella, but Ratzinger has got it right when he talks about Western self-hatred being almost pathological. About how we have to find a way back to our own heritage and our own values [*Ed.:* The reference is probably to the following: "a peculiar Western self-hatred that is nothing short of pathological. It is commendable that the West is trying to be more open, to be more understanding of the values of outsiders, but it has lost all capacity for self-love. All that it sees in its own history is the despicable and the destructive; it is no longer able to perceive what is great and pure," Joseph Ratzinger, now Pope Benedict XVI, in *Without Roots*, 2006, 78 f.].

Interviewer. Doesn't this sort of attitude make it difficult for you to visit other parts of the world, places where they have radically different values, where you'd be on a collision course pretty soon? Although you've traveled a lot, I heard you say a moment ago.

Geraghty. Oh, I get around. But in reality there's bound to be an element of "When in Rome, do as the Romans do". If only for practical reasons. For survival. You can't run about today in Africa and Asia preaching and pontificating the way they did in the colonial era. No wonder missionaries get into so much trouble! On the other hand, if the values you've got mean anything to you, you can't completely deny them. Without your deliberately setting out to provoke anyone, those values of yours need to be there, at least implicitly. The good thing about teaching is that you can *embody* them, so to speak. In the manner in which you present your subject, you reveal yourself as well. "This is the way I am." But sooner or later you'll have what I call *a Martin Luther moment*.

Interviewer. I beg your pardon?

Geraghty. Luther—you know, the Protestant guy?—was called to the Diet of Worms [in 1521—*Ed.*] to face his accusers. He went there under a safe-conduct, but then so did Jan Hus a century earlier [to the Council of Constance in 1415—*Ed.*], and the bastards still burned Hus at the stake. So Marty must have been absolutely shitting himself. Still, he said his piece in front of the emperor, and then he is supposed to have said, "Here I stand. I have no other choice. God help me! Amen." In German, naturally. Or maybe he didn't say it. Only the last four words are reasonably certain. But that doesn't matter, does it? Because whatever his exact words were, they sent out a very clear message. And that sort of integrity, that sort of authenticity, whatever you want to call it, will normally be respected.

Interviewer. Anywhere in the world?

Geraghty. Maybe not. If I went to Saudi Arabia—where I've never been, by the way, it's a terribly *dry* place, in more senses than one—I guess I'd probably have to stay in a touristy culture bubble. [*Laughs*] I do hate having to keep me gob shut! My mother must've been kissing the Blarney Stone when she had me [*Ed.:* Strictly speaking, the ritual of kissing the Blarney

Stone is supposed to endow the *kisser* with "the gift of the gab",
not their offspring].

Interviewer. But you've travelled a lot in the so-called Third
World? India, for example?

Geraghty. I love India, but I stopped going there for years. I
couldn't stand the cruelty, you know, towards women, poor
people, Untouchables, animals. You had to make constant
compromises. Pretend you didn't see things. If you got involved,
tried to stop someone, nobody cottoned what you were doing.
They would look at you and think: "Who's this Irish loony?"
And then, the moment you were gone, they'd go back to whatever nasty business they were doing. Now I could see where
this was coming from. The religious fatalism. The *karma* idea.
You're being punished for being such a shit in your previous
life—and quite rightly too. But simply *understanding* something...does that necessarily equip you to deal with it? This is
a fallacy, let me add, much subscribed to by intellectuals, who
spend most of their time just analyzing things and talking about
them!

Interviewer. Could this explain why you've never settled for
long in a university environment, never been a tenured professor,
only a visiting one, never had an academic career in the formal
sense?

Geraghty. Who would have me?! And I could never put up
with it for long, you know, the petty vanity, the smugness, the
intellectual self-righteousness. Still, you're a university lecturer
yourself, are you not? So maybe we shouldn't go there!
    But to return to what I was saying about standing up for what
you believe in—would you happen to be acquainted with the
fictional works of a certain Thomas Harris?

Interviewer. I'm afraid not.

Geraghty. Well, not to worry. Perhaps you're more familiar with the films derived from Harris's books, focused on a charming character called Hannibal Lecter? I thought so! Anyway, in one of these rather lurid novels the heroine intervenes to try to save the said Hannibal Lecter, a homicidal lunatic incidentally, from being tortured to death by some other psychopath. She says, "The world will not be this way within the reach of my arm" [*Hannibal*, 1999, 488]. To my mind, that's not a bad principle to live by.

Interviewer. "Not on my watch." There's an initiative to fight genocide in Darfur and elsewhere under that name.

Geraghty. Exactly what I mean! Anyhow, over the years I've tried to follow that rule, though cowardice and laziness have often got in the way. If you make too many compromises with your conscience, though, your soul will rot. The fundamentalists, Christian or Muslim—God how I detest them all!—understand this completely. It's we secular types and unbelievers who need to be reminded. In a sense, with our pluralism, our flexibility, in some cases I'm afraid our relativism too, we're like Isaiah Berlin's foxes, and we're up against those chunky monist hedgehogs who aren't going to be easy to push over [*Ed.*: Berlin's famous essay *The Hedgehog and the Fox* was inspired by a fragment by the Greek poet Archilochus, seventh century BC: "The fox knows many things, but the hedgehog knows one big thing"].

Interviewer. You've touched on your Irishness a couple of times. Perhaps I should ask you about that. Is it part of this cultural whatever—heritage, values, tradition—that you say you try to live by?

Geraghty. My Irishness? Begorra, an' top o' of the mornin' to ya! Where's me shamrock? Look—just don't forget what sort of place it is that we Irish call Home. A smallish pile of rocks and bogs stuck out on the edge of Europe, with nothing on one side but the wind and the waves coming in from the Atlantic. In fact, if you go a few miles in *any* direction you'll fall into the sea—and a cold sea at that. And if the Atlantic's not so inviting, what is there on the other side? Who did God in His infinite wisdom give us as neighbors? The fucking Brits! Adding insult to injury, I call it. Ireland's a cold, inhospitable, unforgiving, godawful place most of the year, without much comfort, and if you want to understand the Irish, *that* is what you need to bear in mind: "Gimme shelter."

Do you know *Saint Patrick's Breastplate*—or *The Deer's Cry*, as some people call it? The great prayer of the Irish Dark Ages—well, except they weren't really Dark Ages in Ireland, were they? [*Smiling*] Because we had the Church. It's an appeal for protection: "God's shield to protect me / [...] From every one who shall wish me ill, / Afar and anear, / Alone and in a multitude." Indeed, "against every cruel merciless power that may oppose my body and soul". Christ will be there to shield you: "Christ in the heart of every man who thinks of me" (you hope!), "Christ in the mouth of everyone who speaks of me." It's an absolutely marvellous text, a sort of magic incantation. God will give you shelter, through his Holy Church... but naturally there's a price to pay! And if you're not willing, well then you'll just have to leave Ireland, won't you? Just think of James Joyce and all those other writers who buggered off while they still had the chance!

But there are other kinds of shelter you can take refuge in if you're Irish. There's alcohol. Music. Literature. The crack, even. Why is it that some Irishmen never seem to shut up? Because they're frightened. They're frightened of what would fill the void. And why is our behavior so bloody often *so* emotional, so infantile? Because like small children we desperately want to feel protected, and if that doesn't happen, we kick up a mother of a racket.

Interviewer. Joyce [in *A Portrait of the Artist as a Young Man*,

1916] advocated "silence, exile, and cunning" as the weapons of freedom. Are these routes that *you've* followed?

Geraghty. I can't live in Ireland, though I'm sometimes in Galway, not because of the town, which believe you me is nothing much to write home about, but because of Connemara, and the Aran Islands. Those are places where you can still breathe. And I'm fond of the bookshops in Dublin, especially the second-hand ones. And there's a couple of bars that I like.

Interviewer. Two final questions. Am I allowed to ask you what "T. W." stands for?

Geraghty. Most certainly not.

Interviewer. Come on! Is there any particular reason for the secretiveness?

Geraghty. It's not out of embarrassment, if *that's* what you're hinting at! I'm not Thelonius Wilkes Geraghty or something ridiculous like that. But, you know, where I come from it's still very tribal, and your name reveals your tribe. Now I can't help being named Geraghty, but "Timothy"—that would really mark me as a sodding taig [Catholic—*Ed.*]—and "William" would make me a fucking prod, wouldn't it? Screw them all! A plague on both their sectarian houses!

Interviewer. And—why Liverpool? Why the Adelphi?

Geraghty. It goes back to one of my few slightly longer stints as a university academic, before that particular, highly distinguished institution—no names—realized its awful mistake and mobilized the legal department to get rid of me. I used to tell my young graduate assistants to enjoy their summer breaks, sure, but to meet me without fail on a particular day at the end of the holidays, and in a specific and interesting place. That was before the internet, let alone GoogleMaps, so it wasn't all that easy.

The first year it was at the monastery of Paleokastritsa, on the west coast of Corfu. You know? The palace of Alcinoüs, the father of Nausicaa, was supposedly there, and the bay has the bluest water in the western Mediterranean. This is what [Lawrence] Durrell must have meant by "Somewhere between Calabria and Corfu the blue really begins" [the opening words of Durrell's 1945 book about Corfu, *Prospero's Cell—Ed.*]. I'd been teaching Durrell that term, you see.

The second year it was right here, at the Adelphi. This is a hotel with a lot of history. A century ago, many of the hotel guests would have been passengers waiting to embark on the crossing to America, perhaps on one of the famous steamships of the White Star Line. There's a lounge here which is claimed to be a replica of the First Class Lounge on the *Titanic*. How about that, then!

Interviewer. Though I thought the *Titanic* sailed from Southampton...

Geraghty. Don't spoil the story, lad! Leave it there. [*Pause*] Come on, drink your drink, and think dark thoughts on human destiny!

Interviewer. Well, yes. On which profoundly philosophical note, and before my speech begins to slur too much, we might perhaps end this interview in the time-honoured fashion? [*Raising his glass*] Dr. Geraghty, thank you for your time and patience. I wish you good health, good luck in your future projects, "and may you die in Ireland". I'm sorry, I've forgotten the first part of the toast.

Geraghty. Never mind. Here's another one: "May your glass be ever full / And a strong roof over your head / And may you be safe in Heaven / Before the Devil knows you're dead!"

Because I'd truly hate to be meeting you, next time, not here at the Adelphi but in the, er, downstairs place—which is doubtless where *I'll* be going.

Now, switch the bloody thing off and let's do some proper drinking.

References

Anonymous (probably eighth century, though traditionally attributed to St. Patrick). "The Deer's Cry." Transl. Kuno Meyer. In: *The Penguin Book of Irish Verse*. Ed. Brendan Kennelly. Harmondsworth, Middx.: Penguin, 1970, 45-47.

Berlin, Isaiah. *The Hedgehog and the Fox: An Essay on Tolstoy's View of History* (1953). Revised edition. London: Orion, 1992.

Durrell, Lawrence. *Prospero's Cell: A Guide to the Landscape and Manners of the Island of Corcyra* (1945). London: Faber, 1962.

Harris, Thomas. *Hannibal: A Novel* (1999). Paperback edition. New York: Dell, 2000.

Joyce, James. *A Portrait of the Artist as a Young Man* (1916). Harmondsworth, Middx.: Penguin, 1960.

Ratzinger, Joseph. "The Spiritual Roots of Europe: Yesterday, Today, and Tomorrow." In: Joseph Ratzinger (now Pope Benedict XVI) / Marcello Pera. *Without Roots: The West, Relativism, Christianity, Islam*. Transl. Michael F. Moore. New York: Basic Books, 2006.

Yeats, W[illiam] B[utler]. "The Second Coming" (1919). In: *Yeats's Poems*. Ed. A. Norman Jeffares. London: Papermac, 1989, 294 f.

JAPANESE-AMERICA AS A TRIPLE-HEADED INTERCULTURAL EXPERIENCE

BY SAMAH TAWHID AHMED

AS AN ARAB EGYPTIAN female Other, researching the subject of Japanese-American literature—and interfacing the worlds of both "Japan" and "America"—has been an interesting and personally enriching experience that has broadened the scope of my own cultural horizon. Working at the intersection of diverse yet reconciled settings, and encountering (as a Muslim Egyptian) this interaction through trans-cultural lenses, necessitated my turning to authentic cultural interpreters and typical representatives of second-generation Japanese-America. My materials included two masterpieces of Asian-American popular writing by distinguished authors, John Okada and Monica Sone, news articles and television interviews, and assorted examples of oral history documenting the Japanese experience in the United States. Working with these materials brought an Egyptian researcher into close contact with Japanese-America, resulting in what might be described as a unifying though triple-headed intercultural experience.

In addition to the sources mentioned above, I was also privileged to encounter—albeit in cyberspace—an eminent contemporary representative of Japanese-America, Ken Narasaki. A *sansei* (*i.e.*, third-generation Japanese-American) dramatist, actor and literary manager, he provided me with the script of his stage adaptation of Okada's seminal novel *No-No Boy*, which, supported by a generous grant from the California Civil Liberties Public Education Fund, received its world premiere at the Miles Memorial Playhouse in Santa Monica, California, in 2010.

In tackling *No-No Boy*, the playwright expressed his angry feelings about the ugliness and pervasiveness of the hatred and bigotry faced by his own parents during their years of imprisonment:

> I felt like a bomb had exploded somewhere deep in my soul. I had been rocked to learn about the internment camps and that my parents and their entire families had all been locked up, and had experienced the same kind of frustrations many people of my generation had experienced questioning parents who still felt this experience was better off buried in the past (*No-No Boy*, website).

And Narasaki informed me (in an email correspondence) that "in the aftermath of 9/11, Japanese-Americans were among the first to speak out against racial profiling and the scapegoating of Muslims and Arab Americans".

THE JAPANESE-AMERICAN *nisei* novelist **John Okada** (a *nisei* is a second-generation Japanese-American) was born on September 23rd, 1923, to *issei* parents (*issei* are first-generation Japanese immigrants to the United States). He was raised in the Pioneer Square area of Seattle, WA, where his father Fredy owned a boarding hotel (the old Merchants Hotel). The eldest of three—two brothers and a sister—Okada attended Bailey Gatzert Elementary School and Broadway High School. He was studying at the University of Washington when the Japanese attacked Pearl Harbor, after which event no fewer than 110,000

Americans of Japanese descent were evicted from their homes on the West Coast and transferred to internment camps. Along with the majority of the Seattle Japanese-Americans, the Okada family was shipped first to a segregated center in the interior, Puyallup Fairgrounds. Then they were put on a train to the detention camp center at Minidoka, Idaho.

Okada was among the first group of young *nisei* who volunteered for military duty, where he was assigned to serve as a sergeant in the US Air Force until he was discharged in 1946 (Chen 2000, 281). Afterwards, he went back to Seattle to earn his Bachelor's degrees in English and in Library Science from the University of Washington. It was here that a campus playhouse witnessed the first glimmering of Okada's writing creativity, in the form of a student play that he both wrote and staged. In 1949 he received his Master's degree in English from Teachers College at Columbia University in New York City, where he also met his wife-to-be, Dorothy Arakawa. They married in 1950, and had a daughter and a son.

Okada worked in the Seattle and Detroit Public Libraries. Later, he obtained a job as a technical writer for Chrysler Missile Operations in Sterling Township. Determinedly, he applied himself to the writing of *No-No Boy*. Despite the demands of overtime, and "disrupted vacation plans", he regarded his writing as a "disciplined" avocation and managed to complete the manuscript around 1955 (Ling 1998, 35). Two years later, in 1957, the novel saw the light of day with the help of the Charles E. Tuttle publishing company of Tokyo, who had a strong belief that it would be warmly received by the Japanese-American community to which the author belonged; this, unfortunately, proved not to be the case.

In 1971, Okada, now aged 47, had almost finished the draft of a second novel, about the *issei*, in which he maintained that he had a powerful urge to "faithfully describe the experiences of the immigrant Japanese in the United States before they speedily vanished" (Chen, 281), when he suddenly died. Unluckily, soon after the bereavement "his wife burned the draft of the story about the *issei* in addition to the author's other manuscripts and notes" (*ibid.*). This means that *No-No Boy* is Okada's only surviving work of fiction.

No-No Boy depicts the challenge of defining one's identity in the tension between Japanese nationalist and American assimilationist pressures. The story focuses on Ichiro Yamada, one of the "no-no boys" who refuse to be inducted into the United States armed forces during World War II, and choose prison instead. In other words, he answers "no" to both of the following questions, which were part of the "loyalty questionnaire" given to *nisei* males in the internment camps:

> Question 27: Are you willing to serve in the armed forces of the United States in combat duty, wherever ordered?
>
> Question 28: Will you swear unqualified allegiance to the United States of America and faithfully defend the United States from any or all attack by foreign or domestic forces, and forswear any form of allegiance of obedience to the Japanese Emperor, or to any other foreign government, power or organization? (Collins 1985, 24)

This demand for military service is the fundamental tricky situation described in the narrative, the title of which refers to those *nisei* men who could not resolve the contradiction of being asked to serve in the military of the same nation that had so recently negated their rights both as citizens and as human beings. This gloomy historical stamp left its harrowing impact upon thousands of displaced Japanese-Americans—as well as on Okada's male and female protagonists. Yamada experiences self-contempt and internal racism as a consequence of the way mainstream white culture casts out and demeans the Japanese. This becomes evident through his interior monologs and his interactions with other characters, especially those of his closely-knit community: Ma—Ichiro's mother, Pa—Ichiro's father, Taro—Ichiro's younger brother, Kenji—a wounded 442 veteran, and Freddie—Ichiro's buddy (and a draft resister). By these means the author shows his readers the crisis of identity that Ichiro is undergoing.

Shaped by his continuous pondering over the two ideologies of Japanese nationalism and American assimilationism, Ichiro's estrangement and "craziness" become obvious: "he was the emptiness between the one and the other and could see flashes of truth that was true for his parents and the truth that was true for his brother" (*No-No Boy,* 19). Reduced to this far from favorable binary condition, located between the One (Japanese) and the Other (American), Ichiro thrashes out his duality so as to recover his own chosen identity. Faced with this ethnic binarity, he develops a feeling of abhorrence towards his mother. He sees her as the person who is responsible for his being segregated and displaced. In other words, the one who led him to answer "no" to the two loyalty questions and, hence, to his imprisonment:

> Ma is the rock that's always hammering, pounding, pounding, pounding in her unobtrusive, determined, fanatical way until there's nothing left to call one's self. She's cursed me with her meanness and the hatred that you can not see but which is always hating. It was she who opened my mouth and made my lips move to sound the words which got me two years in prison and an emptiness that is more empty and frightening than the caverns of hell (12).

Stan Yogi (1996) has argued that:

> The choice is false technically, because *nisei* are American by birth. On another level, though, the acceptance of this choice implies that *nisei* adopt a

narrow definition of "American" that excludes them because they are not of European descent (65).

However, in the end it is the figure of Ichiro that suggests a possible beginning to a solution to the problems that arise out of the marginality his *issei* (first-generation) Japanese parents suffered from following their arrival on American soil: to come to terms with the concepts of assimilation and amalgamation in order to secure a place in America, the new homeland. The novel possesses an ending that is really not so much an ending as a beginning, offering a neat completion and resolution to the agony. Ichiro attempts to yoke his own memories of Japan into his new life experience, which begins in Seattle with Emi, his beloved, who represents Ichiro's full integration into American society. In Emi we are given both a nuanced estimation of the incarceration of *nisei* draft resisters and the accommodationist debate that turns a blind eye to US government policy. Over-whelmed by her former "pride" and "patriotism", she recollects those innocent days when—completely dedicated to the red, white, and blue America—she got used to singing the national anthem of the United States at school assemblies. Therefore, Emi's words, avowed afterwards, connote conflicting insights into Ichiro's "choice" when she recommends him to simply "pretend you're back in school":

> Make believe you're singing *The Star-Spangled Ban-ner* and see the color guard march out on the stage and say the pledge of allegiance with all the other boys and girls. You'll get that feeling flooding into your chest and making you want to shout with glory. It might even make you feel like crying. That's how you've got to feel, so big that the bigness seems to want to bust out, and then you'll understand why it is that your mistake was no bigger than the mistake your country made (*No-No Boy*, 96).

By advising him to make believe he's singing *The Star-Spangled Banner* and, basically, admit that he has made a "mistake" by not fighting in the war, Emi shows that she thinks that it is possible for Ichiro to atone for his deeds and make a new start. And her comforting words would lead him to a resolution or healing of that racial exile which at that time was still a distinctive feature of a society like the United States. However, all Emi's efforts cannot erase Ichiro's racial internalization, which breeds even further separation from his Japanese-American family and community in Seattle because he aspires to "keep away from the Japs" (and especially from his parents).

While maintaining an emotive tie to Japanese-American people and the memories of Asian America,

> he walked along, thinking, searching, thinking and probing, and, in the darkness of the alley of the community that was a tiny bit of America, he chased that faint and elusive insinuation of promise as it continued to take shape in mind and heart (251).

The imagery in these words implies the author's adaptation of the model of the "male *Bildungsroman*", as if, after a new period of growing development of his identity, Ichiro will come into view from that dark and narrow alley as a restored and revived new *boy* cleansed of the sins of what went before. His feelings oscillate between total aloofness and a sense of optimism that he can at some point experience the sense of belonging that currently eludes him:

> In time, he thought, in time there will again be a place for me. I will buy a home and love my family and I will walk down the street holding my son's hand and people will stop and talk with us about the weather and the ball games and the elections. I will take my family to visit the family of Freddie [...] and our families together will visit still another family whose father was

two years in the army of America instead of two years in prison and it will not matter about the past, for time will have erased it from our memories and there will be only joy and sorrow and sickness, which is the way things should be (52).

In this way, the second generation's presence in America offered so much promise for assimilation. Thus, Okada attempts to visualize how society may be reborn out of the internal segregated subject being in a racial *state*, and presents his readers with a vision of an America that is in a perpetual process of binding together these racialized subjects. But this conclusion ignores a crucial characteristic of the novel: it ends in the present with Ichiro, the narrator, leaving *Mrs. Yamada's* Seattle community and moving to *American* Seattle. Hence, Ichiro attempts to reconcile or rather create hybrid entities in order to make a more "functional" identity that will serve his own multiple purposes as time passes. Which means that he wants a new life; and he is able to continue with life despite the racial stigma because America is a country which gives ample recognition to other qualities than race. Ichiro hits upon hope in Portland when he applies for a position at an engineering firm—here is the renewed promise of reconstructing his existence. He meets Mr. Carrick, who admits that he "used to have some very good Japanese friends" before the dilemma of internment, an experience which he describes as a "big mistake" made by "the government", and announces that despite this "big black mark in the annals of America's history", this motherland can "still be the best damn nation in the world" (149-50).
Ichiro obtains the position with no further need for an interview, and he perceives that Carrick is seeking to "atone for the error of a big country which hadn't been quite big enough" (151). There seems to be no specific reason for giving *him* the job, however, and Ichiro has doubts about this favoritism that is also, from his point of view, racial pity. He acknowledges that the job properly belongs to "another Japanese who was

equally as American as this man" and in the end does not accept it (*ibid.*). Much like the snowplow that he's building (though there is no snow in Portland), Carrick is unrealistically trying to forge a path towards the promise of a better United States, and away from (though it is something that he himself is blind to) the permanent exceptional status that Ichiro and Japanese-Americans must confront. In his final words, Ichiro questions where he can search for and achieve success: "A glimmer of hope—was that it? It was there, someplace. He couldn't see it to put it into words, but the feeling was pretty strong" (250 f.).

Ichiro's words of hope deserve closer attention. Does he actually accept as true that by saying "yes" to the loyalty questions, he is doing what he "believes" in? Does he really want to fight for, cherish and love the United States? Okada seems to raise such questions through Ichiro's optimistic expectations of being able to find a middle ground between the novel's main competing discourses, namely Japanese nationalism on the one hand and American assimilation on the other. From the world without to the world within, these self-negotiations stress the possibility of Ichiro reaching a sort of neutrality where his Japanese and American halves can be fused into a whole self, just as the conclusion of a "male *Bildungsroman*" ultimately depicts the protagonist's integration into society, which calls for a more or less reconciled acceptance not only of himself but also of the existing social order in general.

Ichiro is also the "forward-looking subject", with a vision of the future that he has from the moment when he announces that he has become excited about the next tomorrow. He gradually withdraws into himself and his own brand new world, and starts thinking positive thoughts that are not related to what is actually happening—for example, after his mother's suicide (by drowning in the bathroom). He decides to forget his former Japanese life, and dresses in no traditional color of mourning for the funeral of his mother, who passed away before her actual physical death, in the sense that she was a legally and socially excluded subject. Ichiro does not have to display grief, but dares to reflect on a future that he believes in, as articulated in his concluding glimmering statement of hope.

Regardless of his determination, the great expectations of the coming days will exert a huge pressure on Ichiro. But this interesting philosophical question is left for the reader to ponder and resolve, in due consideration of the general situation in which Asian-American and other ethnic groups find themselves, beneath the ethnic umbrella of America. Put differently, just being there in a nation state like America involves an unending process of having to authenticate one's existence, with both present and future shaped and determined by America's social and legal system.

The hero is obliged to look at his being in an entirely different light. He can no longer see his Japanese identity as being simply the opposite of his American one; instead, he begins to understand his Japanese and his American identity's values and motivations. An authentic strategy will entail the revision of social and historical prescriptions; familial and community events will be seen from an alternative (positive) viewpoint. There is a clue here as to how Okada can negotiate a path for Ichiro's identity construction. Ichiro claims that he clings to both his American and his Japanese identity. The reader experiences early in the novel how the protagonist hates America, but also realizes that beneath Ichiro's resentment of his mother (who caused him to be sent to prison) and of America (which disregards him as an American citizen) there is a need for love and for connection with a mutually supporting and nurturing Japanese *and* American community. He is complete and healthy enough to be a real "male *Bildungsroman*" hero, and the author's literary technique sustains Ichiro's healthy negotiation of identity.

The consequence is that Ichiro is not so much a "no-no boy" at the end of the novel as someone who is flexible enough to change into a healthy and happy "yes-yes boy". The formation of his identity is full of possibilities derived from two sets of cultural influences. Ichiro accomplishes his negotiation of identity through the establishment of a mutually supporting and informing Japanese-American community.

OKADA DOCUMENTS his protagonist's struggle between the competing forces of his Japanese-American background and his individual identity in the attempt to construct a viable adult persona. In **Monica Sone**'s autobiography *Nisei Daughter* (1953) the focus is likewise on both the inner struggle for identity and the accomplishment of it.

Sone, a talented, second-generation Japanese-American woman author and professional psychologist, was born Kazuko Itoi on December 21st, 1919, in Seattle, WA, to *issei* parents. In his introduction to the 1979 edition of *Nisei Daughter*, S. Frank Miyamoto observes that Sone had an unusual upbringing and that both her parents "appear to have had intellectual and cultural backgrounds well above those of the average *issei*" (xii).

Sone grew up in the Carrollton Hotel, which her mother and father owned and operated in the Pioneer Square district—the city's Skid Row (and the area where John Okada spent his childhood, too)—where she was accustomed to being with people of many different ethnic groups. She was very Americanized, but later learned about Japanese culture and language in a special school that she attended after her normal classes. She visited Japan before World War II broke out and enjoyed the experience, but she felt as though she were an American foreigner there, and longed to get back to her Seattle home.

When Kazuko returned, she planned to resume her life, but on December 7th, 1941, the Japanese attacked Pearl Harbor, and her life was turned upside down. Later, Sone earned a Bachelor's degree from Hanover College in southern Indiana and a Master's in clinical psychology at the Case Western Reserve University in Cleveland. She married Geary Sone and raised four children in Canton, Ohio, where she worked as a clinical psychologist.

Mary Young says that Sone's experiences as a *nisei* female were different from those of *nisei* males. As a woman, she could not (like John Okada) join the Army and by so doing prove her loyalty. Instead, she worked as a stenographer, which was traditional female work, maintaining the records of interned Japanese and Japanese-Americans (1625). Kazuko, the protagonist of the autobiography, provides a unique personal account of a young *nisei* female whose childhood, adolescence, and young womanhood are chronicled before, during, and after the bombing of Pearl Harbor that led to her internment together with her Japanese family. The narrative is dedicated to the pre-war life, specifically the period of childhood "described as blissful and innocent, but also overshadowed by some incidents of cultural conflict and racial tension" (Huang 2005).

Kazuko and her family endured relocation, and were accommodated in internment camp cells. During the mid-Forties, the War Relocation Authority decided to open their barbed wired camp gates to both male and female *nisei*, who could therefore go out in search of a new life and viable identity. One such launching ticket (for Chicago) was offered to Kazuko. Later, there was the liberal arts college in southern Indiana. But she came to realize that merging into mainstream American society, bearing with her the Japanese ancestral identity of her *issei* parents, was as difficult as her attempt to remain "invisible".

The narrator's attitude is made clear at the end of the text, when she tells her parents how she came to discover that "the Japanese and the American parts of [her] were now blended into one" (*Nisei Daughter*, 238):

> I don't resent my Japanese blood anymore. I am proud of it, in fact, because of you and the *issei* who've struggled so much for us. It's really nice to be born into two cultures, like getting a real bargain in life, two for the price of one. The hardest part, I guess, is the growing up, but after that, it can be interesting and stimulating. I used to feel like a two-headed monstrosity, but now I find that two heads are better than one (236).

Her "favorable outlook"—which entailed assimilating into the dominant culture that had intentionally supported her segregation and stripped her of her right to American citizenship—is the strategic resolution that Kazuko San resorted to. Being Japanese and American was no longer seen as a crisis for the protagonist to accept and even to live with. Critic Traise Yamamoto has something to say about this hopeful view: "this optimist veneer is really a carefully engineered performance, which allows the *nisei* woman narrator to educate non-Asian readers about the internment without offending them" (quoted in Huang).

Kazuko's "divided narrative voice" nuances in subtle ways— interwoven with irony and understatement—so as to reveal the tensions surrounding Japanese-American identity formation shaped by the specific traumatic moments of internment and assimilationist pressures. Sone's use of autobiography is a strategic way of writing. The genre is not solely a means to write about her personal female experience as an Asian-American woman living amid racial hatred toward the Japanese in the United States and her own experiences of identity or female subjectivity that is continually being defined, redefined, and "transformed". Sone also manipulates this genre to produce a kind of open debate in which she can articulate her personal feelings about the racial discrimination that she and other Japanese individuals had to encounter in the United States of the twentieth century.

According to Caren Kaplan (1992):

> Out-law genres renegotiate the relationship between personal identity and the world, between personal and social history. Here narrative inventions are tied to a struggle for cultural survival rather than purely aesthetic experimentation or individual expression (130).

However, the two writers, Sone and Okada, use differing strategies that effectively represent the difficulty involved in negotiating the competing tensions of their Japanese-American identity, surrounded as it is with social and political context that has a direct bearing on that negotiation.

It is interesting to note the reception given to these two texts by the critics. According to Jinqi Ling, Sone's memoir was "the most important Japanese-American literary work published in the 1950s prior to *No-No Boy*". Moreover, the autobiography "became an instant commercial success for its mainstream publisher", presumably because, in his opinion, "it satisfied what the age demanded of the Japanese American literary voice", which included "explanations of the exotic but nonthreatening otherness of Japanese-American life to mainstream readers, and accounts of successful transition into the mainstream" (36).

On the other hand, Okada's book was largely ignored. As Ling remarks:

> The literary establishment's rejection of *No-No Boy* was followed by a period of silence about representations of the internment in Japanese-American novels, presumably because the rejection discouraged further marketing of politically sensitive Japanese-American literary works by large commercial presses (50).

He added that it was not until the second half of the Seventies that the internment was brought up again openly as a constitutional issue through the redress movement led by the Japanese American Citizens League (JACL), whose efforts contributed greatly to the passing of the Civil Liberties Act of 1988, which issued an official apology to Japanese-Americans who had been interned and provided funds for surviving internees in reparation for their losses during the war (51). At about the same time as former internees began to seek redress for their war time sufferings, Okada's novel was coming to be seen as a major classic of Asian American writing. The author—who "died in obscurity believing that Asian America had rejected the book" (back cover of the novel)—would have been thrilled if he could have witnessed the overwhelming recent success of his work. Particularly if he had learned that it has invaded American cultural courses and has been adapted for the theater by a typical representative of Japanese-American ancestry.

DESPITE THE DYNAMIC intercultural role played by international conferences and cultural councils throughout Egypt, ethnicity-specific courses offered by the English departments of Egyptian universities tend to deal only with African-American issues. Not one single Asian-American text (for instance) is integrated into American literature courses. In my own experience, courses that *do* explore ethnic American culture focus on literature from just that one ethnicity, and a text by an African-American—such as the much celebrated and frequently studied contemporary American author, the Pulitzer and Nobel Prize winner Toni Morrison—will typically be compared only with texts by other African Americans.

The exceptional pleasure of having an interfacing discourse between works from different heritages—Arab-, Armenian-, Chinese-, Filipino-, Indian-, Iranian-, Korean-, Pakistani- or Japanese-American, to name just a few of the "hyphenated American" possibilities—is, unfortunately, never realized. Above and beyond retracing how it came to be valued for being representative of a large body of work of ethnic American writing, communicating "Japanese-America" motivates careful analysis of dual culture through social or political similarities that would give new life to a curriculum that is often rather unadventurous.

What I would suggest is this: *to compare very diverse cultural experiences within the larger context of American multicultural courses and American studies in general, demonstrating how American texts of different cultural origins confront similar shared issues, albeit in varying historical contexts.*

This could be achieved if students were encouraged to set these multicultural voices, including their own, in a dialog with one another, leading to a proper understanding of common aims and problems that bring together and separate dissimilar types of people. Students are often ideal candidates to serve as perceptive mediators between their own culture and that (or those) of the Other. By studying and motivating a focus for teaching Asian-American culture, for example, Egyptian students will come to cross various cultural paths, and by crossing paths achieve a better perception of their own and others' ethnicity.

In a television interview in 2006, the Egyptian literary critic and English professor Gamal Abdel Nasser discussed the issue of familiarization with the Other. Arguing strongly for the idea that students can better comprehend and understand different cultures when they are familiar with one or more languages beside their own (a view emphatically supported by teachers of English language), Dr. Abdel Nasser had this to say about the students' cultural backgrounds:

> You [English language students] have the ability to view the world through both eyes, whereas students who do not learn additional languages view the world through one eye; the meaning of this being that multilingual students can better switch between cultures, and therefore are better equipped to translate texts. The imperative for students is to be both multicultural and multilingual (my own translation).

The arguments for "multicultural and multilingual" learning are compelling. Students have not only the chance to enter unexplored worlds, but also to read and learn about the thoughts of the Other. This means that it is crucial for everyone to know another language so that he or she can commune through this language with a different culture. Abdel Nasser proceeds to develop a notion that evaluates specific forms of knowledge when he goes further into the concept of a dialog that takes into account the mutual nature of a definite area of cultural ignorance or knowledge.

A start has indeed been made at some universities, but if undergraduates are to fulfil the cultural requirements of life in the twenty-first century, colleges and universities throughout the country must focus more attention on multicultural studies.

As I have already mentioned, for years now the educational curriculum has tended to be unadventurous—and decidedly monocultural.

To begin with, the student who sets out to scrutinize another nation's culture must approach—for instance—its written records with sensitivity and a willingness to appreciate any related piece of work, history, literature, fiction, *etc*. However, such a process of intensive reading as will enrich his or her imagination cannot be achieved without the help of the library. A corpus of ethnic cultural studies is needed if the student is to be enabled to find the answers to questions posed by the text.

Unfortunately, finding sources, whether primary or secondary, here in Egypt is often a major problem, especially when you are based in a small college some distance from the capital. While researching my own project, for example, I had to travel from my city to Cairo—120 km—on an almost daily basis in order to use the secondary sources available at the American University Library (AUC). In difficult cases, perhaps once a month, I would travel to Alexandria, to use the fine modern successor to what was, in ancient Greek and Roman times, the greatest library in the world.

By whatever means I could, I probed further to bring my Arab-Egyptian identity into closer interface with the double-headedness of "Japanese-America".

Accessing audio-visual materials created by American and Asian-American filmmakers about the Japanese-American internment experience was scarcely less important than getting to grips with the written sources. There is, for instance, the eclectic *Lest We Forget,* the award-winning documentary by Jason DaSilva, which combines the personal accounts of those who have felt the severity of wartime racism, both past and present, and does it in a very disciplined manner. It contains both vintage and recent film footage, and convincing inter-views not only with Japanese-American internment camp residents and camp officials, but also with Americans of other cultural backgrounds, such as Middle Easterners and South

Asians, permitting further transcultural interface with the Other. It corroborates the aim of this present paper, in that it adds many useful insights to my own understanding of how we are locked into cultural perception by our particular perspective, and includes such parallels as that between the treatment of Japanese-Americans in World War II and the (supposed) persecution—much exaggerated in the world media—of Middle Easterners and South Asians after 9/11. And, as Lawson Fasao Inada (2005) says (in the context of narrative history), "as with anything else, its effect depends on what you bring to it" (204).

The interviews with internment camp victims highlight how they sensed profound changes in the status of their Japanese-American family and community as a whole, especially as regarding their then-emerging sense of identity. Particular attention is given to the journey of self-discovery, especially when this journey tends to reflect an attempt at self-recovery and functions as a means of emphasizing their embattled Japanese identity within the confines of its American diaspora.

As THE CULTURAL THEORIST Stuart Hall (1990) has argued:

> Cultural identities come from somewhere, have histories. But, like everything which is historical, they undergo constant transformation. Far from being externally fixed in some essentialist past, they are subject to the continuous "play" of history, culture and power. Far from being grounded in mere "recovery" of the past, which is waiting to be found, and which when found, will secure our sense of our selves into eternity, identities are the names we give to the different ways we are positioned by, and position ourselves within, the narratives of the past (225).

"Cultural identities come from somewhere." Or to put it another way, how do we reach a particular state of possessing an identity? Our identity, or the "I" inside each of us, needs to be conceived as clearly "articulated", given that "what we say is always 'in context', positioned" (222). The "subject" is thus in constant process of transformation. The question of how identities are "articulated", "demolished", "recovered" or "constructed" within particular historical moments—this is what calls us forth to cross the borders of "Japanese-America", say, to become, in the end, triple-headed cultural interlocutors, piecing together a different meaning to our existence.

References

Abdel Nasser, Gamal. Interview [in Arabic] with Nahid Salem on the TV program *Banat afkari* ["Fresh Thoughts"]. Egyptian Radio and Television Union, Channel 2, Cairo, June 29th, 2006.

Chen, Fu-jen. "John Okada (1923-1971)." In: *Asian American Novelists: A Bio-Bibliographical Critical Sourcebook*. Ed. Emmanuel S. Nelson. Westport, CT: Greenwood Press, 2000, 281-88.

Collins, Donald E. *Native American Aliens: Disloyalty and the Renunciation of Citizenship by Japanese Americans during World War II*. Westport, CT: Greenwood Press, 1985.

Hall, Stuart. "Cultural Identity and Diaspora" (1990). Website, <http://www.unipa.it/~michele.cometa/hall_cultural_ identity.pdf>

Huang, Shuchen Susan. "Monica Sone." In: *The Greenwood Encyclopedia of Multiethnic American Literature*. Volume 4: N-S. Ed. Emmanuel S. Nelson. Westport, CT: Greenwood Press, 2005, 2061.

Inada, Fasao Lawson. "Books & the Arts: Ghostly Camps, Alien Nation." In: *The Nation*, August 28th-September 4th, 2005, 204-11.

Kaplan, Caren. "Resisting Autobiography: Out-Law Genres and Transnational Feminist Subjects." In: *De/colonizing the Subject: The Politics of Gender in Women's Autobiography*. Ed. Sidonie Smith / Julia Watson. Minneapolis, MN: University of

Minnesota Press, 1992, 115-38.

Lest We Forget. Dir. Jason DaSilva. Canada/USA, 2003.

Ling, Jinqi. *Narrating Nationalisms: Ideology and Form in Asian American Literature.* New York: Oxford University Press, 1998.

Miyamoto, S. Frank. "Introduction." In: Monica Sone. *Nisei Daughter* (1953). Seattle, WA: University of Washington Press, 1979.

No No Boy 2010. Website, <http://sites.google.com/site/nonoboyplay/about-the-playwrite>

Okada, John. *No-No Boy* (1957). Seattle, WA: University of Washington Press, 2001.

Sone, Monica. *Nisei Daughter* (1953). Seattle, WA: University of Washington Press, 2000.

Yogi, Stan. "You Had To Be One or the Other: Oppositions and Reconciliation in John Okada's *No-No Boy.*" In: *MELUS*, 21, 2, summer 1996, 63-77.

Young, Mary. *"Nisei Daughter."* In: *MasterPlots II* (Women's Literature Series). Ed. Frank N. Magill. Volume 4. Pasadena, CA: Salem Press, 1995, 1622-25.

RE-IMAGINING THE
NOTION OF HOME

METAPHORS OF MEMORY IN
THE POETRY OF RANJIT HOSKOTÉ
BY CLAUS TELGE

FROM MARCH TO June 2002, the Wiener Kunsthalle hosted the exhibition *Capital & Karma—Recent Positions in Indian Art*, displaying the works of such artists as Atul Dodiya, Subodh Gupta and Ranbir Kaleka. As stated in the Preface of the exhibition catalog, the contemporary Indian artists participating in the exhibition "apply in their work Indian and Western elements as equally important resources", weaving together "popular culture" and "traditional motifs" (11). In her own contribution to the catalog, curator Angelika Fitz depicts India as a historical invention, referring to remarks made by the British historian E. P. Thompson:

> All the convergent influences of the world run through this society: Hindu, Moslem, secular, liberal, Marxist, democratic socialist, Gandhian. There is not a thought that is being thought in West or East which is not active in some Indian mind (60).

India has been "a screen for projections" (*ibid.*) of many European intellectuals and politicians. Since it gained independence in 1947, India has undergone various social and cultural transformations, the last being the so called "economic liberalization" of the Nineties. It is this context which frames the exhibition's theme, as explained by the Bombay-born poet, art critic, cultural theorist and independent curator Ranjit Hoskoté in his follow up reflections on contemporary Indian art. He paints the picture of a generation that is critically adapting "globalization as a neo-colonial process of co-option and as a process of emancipation" (37), constantly displacing old and new screens of projections in the search for identity. I will elaborate on this later.

It is also this "reception and transmission" (11) of culture, either foreign or local, that sets the stage for Hoskoté's poetry, in which he intertwines competing knowledge discourses and different belief systems, encountering the Other in the interplay of memory, identity and poetic language. I have to admit being very surprised when *Die Ankunft der Vögel* (2006b), the first volume of poetry by Ranjit Hoskoté translated into German, fell into my hands in a small bookshop in Prenzlauer Berg in Berlin. Glancing through "Leonardo", the book's first poem, I immediately sensed something that felt different from what the average interested German reader like myself would expect of a "typical" Indian poet.

According to Hoskoté's friend the German-Bulgarian writer Ilija Trojanow (2001), it is very unlikely that you will find any orientalisms or traditional forms like the *ghazal* in his poems. Instead, "Leonardo" takes the reader to Tuscany, evoking imagery of the fine arts. The poem makes direct reference to a famous passage from Da Vinci's notebook, the so-called *Codex Atlanticus*, in which Da Vinci recalls an early childhood memory. As he was lying in a cradle, a hawk came in, opening his mouth with its tail, and sticking it several times inside his lips: "Vulture [...] misheard bird [...] fluttering at my mouth" (see Andersen 2001, 4). Interestingly, the line in the poem goes back to Freud's interpretation of the passage in *Leonardo da Vinci and a Memory of His Childhood* (1910), which he based on a mistranslation of the Italian *nibio* (hawk) as "vulture". This bird was obviously "misheard". More and more the reader is presented with the image of an erudite author who appears to be well read in European intellectual history. Reading further into his work, one quickly discovers that references to the Western intellectual tradition are juxtaposed with imagery and mythologies of the poet's homeland, as in these lines taken from the poem "Trailing the Horse-tamer" (in *The Sleepwalker's Archive*, 2001): "I stumble into a widowed wood / where trees born of women / have suffered the knives of drought" (76). Trojanow acknowledges that this shows a confident and natural eclectic self-will.

This is also reflected in the next thing which caught my attention that day. The poems I was reading were translated from English, and, as can be assumed, Indian poetry has a rather ambivalent relationship to the English language. Hoskoté, born in 1969, belongs to a generation of postcolonial Indian poets writing in English who began publishing in the late Eighties, and who did not have to fight the ideological battles of their literary predecessors. Older poets like Nissim Ezekiel, Adil Jussawalla or Dom Moraes came from a rather secular, urban and bourgeois background and were influenced by a modernist Western and English-speaking literary tradition. On the one hand, they had to step out of the shadow of the old W. B. Yeats paradigm that "no man can think or write with music and vigor except in his mother tongue" (1937, see Patke 2006, 60); "Indo-Anglian" poetry was a "blind alley, lined with curio shops, leading nowhere" (Walsh 1990, 127). On the other hand, they had to face the postcolonial advocates of the "nativist argument", claiming that "encouraging a foreign language system to be a fit medium for creative writing" would bring the "already low-value culture still lower" (Marathi novelist Balchandra Nemade, quoted in Patke, 60). But, finally, these poets paved the way for authors like Hoskoté who are now using the language of the former colonizers without any feelings of guilt or inferiority.

In his anthology *Reasons for Belonging: Fourteen Contemporary Indian Poets* (2002), Hoskoté describes his generation as being able to be "situated without being rooted, able to travel without getting lost" (xiv). They are "at home in a world in which the boundary between the local and the global has increasingly been blurred", and "they wrestle with the ethical and artistic dilemmas produced by such a blurring" (*ibid.*). Their writing derives from the urban perception of India's integration into the globalized world and the economic, social, cultural and symbolic transformations that come with that. However, according to Hoskoté, they "do not subscribe to a collective avant-garde aesthetic" (*ibid.*). They critically embrace the given conditions of India's cultural hybridity, a concept coined by postcolonial theorist Homi K. Bhabha (1994), in which identity is perceived as a processual and performative construction and not as a fixed entity. According to Bhabha, cultural hybridity "gives rise to [...] a new area of negotiation of meaning and representation" (Rutherford 1990, 211). This process takes place in a "third space of enunciation" that challenges our "sense of the historical identity of culture as a homogenizing, unifying force, authenticated by the originary Past, kept alive in the national tradition of the People" (Bhabha, 54).

And yet—the fact that Hoskoté is writing in English creates a certain tension. In India, a country so enormously rich in languages, English is a secondary official language, but also exists as a form of Hindi-English, which varies locally. The literary English that we find in Hoskoté's poetry is spoken only by a privileged elite, mostly educated in Europe and the United States. This linguistic gesture should not be misunderstood as a yearning for belonging to Western discourse, but rather as an expression of literary self-confidence. For Hoskoté, the poet should be free to distance himself from any essentialist or modernist folklore, regardless of whichever place he is looking at the world from. However, the colonial experience stays present in his poetry. Thus, Hoskoté can be called a postcolonial poet as, according to Rajeev S. Patke's (2006) general definition of postcolonial poetry, his poems display "awareness of what it means to write from a place and in a language shaped by colonial history, at a time that is not yet free from the force of that shaping" (6). In his writing, the shaping of language even becomes an archeological enterprise in which prehistoric and present time overlap.

The third stanza of "Trailing the Horse-tamer" presents a primordial scene in central Asia: "From the steaming belly of the sacrificed ox / the augur pulls the looped entrails". Then, the poem reaches out into the present. The "Horse-tamer" is asked to "sharpen" the "frost-bitten stumps of [...] language", making an appeal to poetry to make time-transcending transformations of language accessible for the present. A similar archetypal notion is conveyed in the poem "Speaking a Dead Language" (in *The Sleepwalker's Archive* 2001) in which the "cadences" of a dead language are "learned again / in other countries by other tongues" (152).

According to Jürgen Brôcan, Hoskoté's German translator, the concept of language that we find here is not self-referential. It is a celebration of the poetic metaphor as an archaic way of acquiring knowledge. In his Afterword to *Die Ankunft der Vögel*, Brôcan draws parallels between Hoskoté's way of writing and painting. In "Leonardo", which originally appeared in Hoskoté's debut *Zones of Assault* (1991), a poetological metaphor emerges that can be applied to both painting and writing: "the brush fleshes the impossible / as it lands from what could not be / on the strand of what has been made." As in painting, the world (or "the impossible") takes shape and becomes sensually perceivable in poetry. Also, he often touches in his poems and essays on European painters like Francis Bacon or Anselm Kiefer, and also, of course, on Indian painters like Atul Dodiya, Laxman Shreshtha or Jehangir Sabavala.

In a presentation given at the General Meeting of the International Association of Residential Arts Centers in New Delhi in 1998, entitled *Beyond the House of Wonders: Some Remarks on the Possibility of Inter-cultural Communication*, Hoskoté talked about contemporary Indian artists struggling to find an aesthetic and ethical position in the process of globalization and fragmentation which had deeply affected India. Hoskoté was not only speaking as an art critic or cultural theorist, but also as a poet. I therefore read some passages as poetological statements, juxtaposing his way of writing with his thoughts on the condition of Indian art.

In the last chapter, Hoskoté explores the question of how an Indian artist can imagine a notion of home, that is, a space of identification, independently of the cultural hegemony of "western contemporaneity [...], the [...] up-to-date modernity via the authorized New York-London-Paris-Berlin route" (Hoskoté, 1998), as well as the cultural forces of Indian nationalism and its politics of national identity. Therefore, he postulates the strategy that "[c]ontemporary Indian artists continuously re-imagine their notion of home and homeland" (*ibid.*). As in Bhabha's figure of the third space, the imaginary of identity and belonging is constantly renegotiated, producing new cultural symbols and meaning. In the following, I will elaborate on the practice of this strategy by analyzing Hoskoté's use of meta-phors of memory. Both of the aforementioned characteristics of his writings, the primacy of image and the intertwining of the past and the present, are embodied in the ways in which the post-colonial consciousness in his poems—a consciousness that is aware of "the old colonialism that globalization perpetu-ates and the new colonialism that it [globalization] enforces" (*ibid.*)—shapes memory and is shaped by memory. The forma-tive force of this shaping of identity emerges from the process of re-imagining the notion of home.

According to Aleida Assmann (1991), one cannot talk about memories without using metaphors. Metaphors are "figures of thought" (13, my translation) which allow us to access the "subject of memoria" (Butzer 2005, 13, my translation). Together with her husband Jan Assmann (Assmann / Czaplicka 1995) she coined the term "cultural memory", "a collective concept for all knowledge that directs behavior and experience in the interac-tive frame-work of a society and one that obtains through gener-ations in repeated societal practice and initiation" (126). One of the oldest forms of cultural memory is remembering the dead, which is initiated in numerous dedicated poems by Hoskoté. In her book *Erinnerungsräume: Formen und Wandlungen des kulturellen Gedächtnisses* (1999), Aleida Assmann develops an imagery of memory that I will use to analyze the interplay between memory and identity in "A Poem for Grandmother".

As Brôcan writes in his Afterword to *Die Ankunft der Vögel*, the titles of Hoskoté's volumes of poetry as well as his poems function as coordinates for framing the whole text. They point to the key topics around and out of which he develops his poems. "A Poem for Grandmother" is from *The Sleepwalker's Archive*. The title of the book introduces an architectural imagery of memory, articulating the cultural function of the archive for collective and personal identity. In Harald Weinrich's *Typen der Gedächtnismetaphorik* (1964)—on which Assmann based her work—the archive is a building metaphor that represents the storage capacity of memory, *i.e.*, an accumulation of, for example, texts, images and films, which form a collective material repository of shared cultural knowledge that shapes and sustains cultural identity. The archive can also function as an instrument of political authority, asserting power and control over cultural memory. In contrast, in the *Archaeology of Knowledge* (2002) Michel Foucault defines the archive as an immaterial instrument of constraint, as the "law of what can be said", which is not that which "safeguards the event of the statement, and preserves, for future memories, its status as an escapee; it is that which, at the very root of the statement-event, and in that which embodies it, defines at the outset the system of enunciability" (146).

In the title of Hoskoté's collection, both the material and immaterial features of the archive metaphor are contrasted with the appearance of the archive's owner: the sleepwalker. Remembering is a mental cognitive construction which has to become conscious and can then be articulated through language (Nünning 2004, 217), whereas the sleepwalker acts in a liminal space between dream and reality, while still perceiving his environment unconsciously. A body-bound memory formation is taking place, which is not transferred into accessible memory outside the bodily dimension. As pointed out by Rudolf Heinz and Christoph Weismüller (1996), somnambulism is a "*paradox*-differential existence of the real in the sense of [...] vain resistance against its representation" (22, my translation, emphasis in the original). Relating this to the metaphor of the archive, the shaping of memory is located in the field of the third space, where overlapping collective memories are de- and recontextualised. Such an archival form of writing, as Libbie Rifkin (2000) writes, does not as in Foucault's or Weinrich's concept of the archive "constrain writerly agency", it is more like an "extension [...] of it" (12). *The Sleepwalker's Archive* serves as a poetological metaphor that reflects the opening of an imaginary space of representation, within which Hoskoté eclectically intertwines transcultural memories.

In addition to this rather floating and fragmented writing of archival memory, one also finds a personal moment of keeping and remembrance in the metaphor of the volume's title:

> The idea of the archive has always been strong in my work, and that became intensified in *The Sleepwalker's Archive*. I found myself confronted by the fear of the loss of memory, the loss of language. This fear was shaped by factors as diverse as friend and poet Nissim Ezekiel's struggle with Alzheimer close at hand, as well as the destruction of the Bamiyan Buddhas in a more global context (Subramaniam 2005).

Ultimately, in its paradox, the figure of the sleepwalker refers to mortality. Heinz and Weismüller describe somnambulant behaviour in deep sleep as "the animation of death on the living body" (36, my translation). This moment of fear and loss brings in a different accentuation of Bhabha's third space, namely the spiritual yearning for a safe place within one's own culture in the sense of belonging. For Hoskoté (2000a) this place is the poem itself: "in the continuous war of positions that is contemporary life, the poem is a liberated zone; it is the only real homeland that the poet can claim" (xxvi).

Such a place can be found in "A Poem for Grandmother" (2001). Hoskoté presented it to the public as a stipendiary of the International Writing Programs at the University of Iowa in the fall of 1995. It remains unclear whether he actually wrote the poem in Iowa. It is more likely that it originated during a creative period in 1994 when Hoskoté involved himself with the works of the seventeenth-century Indian poet and saint Tukaram in the town of Dehu. The years after his debut collection *Zones of Assault* (1991) had been very difficult and for a while he "did wonder whether the poetic impulse had left him altogether" (Subramaniam). Dehu and Iowa marked a turning point in his creative struggle and much of *The Cartographer's Apprentice* (2000a), a collaboration with painter Laxman Shrestha, and *The Sleepwalker's Archive* (2001) emerged from that period. Nevertheless, nine years had passed before *The Cartographer's Apprentice* came out in 2000, years in which the Indian poet also worked as an art critic for *The Times of India*, wrote a study of the modern Indian painter Jehangir Sabavala, and co-translated Marathi poet Vasant Abaji Dahake into English.

For Hoskoté, working with Shrestha was an "occasion to test-run" his longer poems, "which had until then neither a reading nor a publishing context" (Subramaniam). In fact, a number of poems such as "Speaking a Dead Language" appeared in both books, *The Cartographer's Apprentice* as well as *The Sleepwalker's Archive*. The "test-run" showed that there had been a shift in his writing, away from the ciphered and alienated language of *Zones of Assault*, which deliberately held the voice of the poem in suspense, to an articulate self that locates itself in a historical frame of reference, as in "A Poem for Grandmother". According to Hoskoté, the poem not only refers to India's colonial past, but also follows an autobiographical impulse without fully making it the center of the poem, though:

Some of these poems, actually, center on the colonial experience and draw energy of a certain kind from it. [...] The next few poems have to do, well, really with my grandparents who were part of [...] the colonial past. So hopefully, these poems are an attempt to look back, not only at my family, but also at that phase in history in which they were active participants (from the 1995 interview with Clark Blaise).

Remembering his grandparents becomes an interweaving of family and world history, within which the subject of the text oscillates between past and present in a somnambulant-like state, creating its own system of reference. Even though the dedication in the title of the poem signals an autobiographical and emotional relationship, it should not hastily be read as an author's posthumous homage to his grandmother. Dedicating poems to friends or other artists, such as the famous Indian poet Nissim Ezekiel in "Passing a Ruined Mill" (2006a) or the German painter Anselm Kiefer in "Zweistromland" (1991), is a genre that Hoskoté makes use of quite often. Again, as he himself says, it is more his aim of setting the self in "a historical framework, without letting it turn autobiographical in a maudlin or confessional manner" (Subramaniam).

According to Jan Assmann (2005), remembering the dead is the most pure and widespread form of cultural memory. The irreversible loss of life is turned into a form of past life memories, within which the immediate family members remember and uphold the memory of the deceased, keeping them as a member of their community and taking them along with them in the continuing present (34). The titles of the dedicated poems not only point to this universally ritualized form of remembrance, but also shift the significance of the lyric genre's memory function from a textual to a metatextual level.

In his essay "Literarische Gattungen und Gedächtnis" (2005), Richard Humphrey writes that poetry is one of the literary genres which "occupies the relation between literature and memory most intensively" (85, my translation here and in the following quotations from Humphrey). He grounds this assumption in its use of classical mnemotechniques such as metrics, rhyme, rhythm and tropes. In his lecture "A Poet's Creed" (1967), Jorge Luis Borges defines words "as symbols for shared memories" (117) and, according to Humphrey, the lyric genre enhances them so that they become an almost ideal communicator of memory. However, in his eyes, the frame of memory of poetry is rather "small" and "fine" (85 f.). Its essence is a rather "delicate net of memory, which catches personal experiences and inwardness" (85), as exemplified by the "poetry of feeling and experience"—he quotes such poems as Edward Thomas's "Adlestrop" ("Yes. I remember Adlestrop") and Christina Rossetti's famous sonnet "Remember" ("Remember me when I am gone away") (86).

This way of writing poetry certainly has its place, but Humphrey's generalizing notion of the lyrical self's horizon of memory as "small" and "fine" is rather problematic—and, especially in our context, simply inadequate for describing memory processes in postcolonial poetry. When Hoskoté spoke of introducing a historical self to his work, that also implied a stronger incorporation of narrative, autobiography and epic. His poems are not bound to a momental and fixed reservoir of memories; instead (to stay with Humphrey's metaphor of the net) they constantly create new nodes of memory.

"A Poem for Grandmother"—the complete text can be found online on several websites—stretches such a net of memories, while at the same time reflecting on the memory function of poetry.

It begins

A Poem for Grandmother

A door. A stair. And two steps inside that dark,
the straight-backed chair my grandmother sat in,
a lace net draped across its mahogany arm.

And on the table, a volume of stories
open at the flyleaf, its tissue quill-scarred.

The transition from the title of the poem to the first stanza
suspends the usual formal difference between title and stanza. I
tentatively read it as a one line listing: "A Poem (for Grandmother).
A door. A stair. And two steps inside that dark." On one level,
the self enters a room of memory, symbolized by the door as a
space of transition. After passing the stairs, there is darkness.
The figure of the sleepwalker shines through again. It is this state
of being in the dark, a place without light and life, out of which
the process of remembering is initiated. On another level, this
transitional phase locates the poem as a place of remembrance.
I have put the dedication "for Grandmother" in brackets, as it
concretizes the memory function of the poem: remembering a
deceased relative. The room that is entered contains objects that
once surrounded the grandmother: "the straight-backed chair,
a lace net, a volume of stories." The shiny brown mahogany
of the chair gives the room a melancholy feeling of nostalgia.
Its earthy tone also signals the presence of primordial motherly
energy. However, the *Dictionary of Symbols and Imagery* (de
Vries, 1973) ascribes a "Victorian lack of emotion and spirituality" (66) to this piece of mahogany furniture. The ambiguous
symbolism of the object juxtaposes a warm domestic space
with a cold and rational Victorianism. The "volume of stories"
lying on the table represents the "mimesis of memory", *i.e.*, the
literary representations of individual and cultural memory (see
Neumann 2008). Therefore, the metaphoric compound word
"quill-scarred" can be read as a commentary on this textual
/ metatextual allusion, as it anthropomorphizes the writing
process by incorporating a particular feature of the memory of
the body. Certain memories are physically memorized through
pain and leave scars on the body, which in this context can be
read as a metaphor of writing. The quill is successively carving
wounds, heaping layers of memory. This process of remembering is painful. And, as Aleida Assmann (1999) points out,

inflicting pain can be a very efficient mnemotechnique, not only regarding biographical memory, but also, in line with Nietzsche and Foucault, as a reinforcement of collective memory with institutionalized practices of "discipline and punish" (241 *et seq.*). In the postcolonial context of the poem, this wounded body of writing embodies the presence of the former colonial power—the literary net of memories is a scar tissue.

As the first stanza ends with a body metaphor of memory of writing, we find another one of its derivates in the second, namely analog photography, which can also be classified as a "phenomenon of bodily imprinting" (247, my translation). The photographic process of imprinting goes back to real life events which leave traces on the photo material, sealing the grandmother "in a shell of relations." Also, the shell—a symbol that one finds quite often in Hoskoté's poems—takes on the notion of motherly love, showing the grandmother contented and secure amidst her family. She resembles Lakshmi, the Hindu goddess of beauty, who is closely associated with the fertility imagery of water, shell and pearl. Lakshmi's powers are tamed by marriage, and she stands for gentleness, harmony and wealth (Erndl 1993, 154). This idealization leads to a dreamlike scene where the poetic self imagines his grandmother as an empress, "accepting tributes of porcelain and sparkling brass". The color of the "sepia corset" carries over the nostalgic atmosphere from the first stanza, while at the same time its Victorian connotation foreshadows the revelation of the presented scene as grotesque projection of the colonial power, which is portrayed in the third stanza as "invalids who ruled from brass-bound chests and serene beds of illness", the grandmother being their servant. With the line "the wrong word kills, and *empress* is wrong", the underlying presence of the British Raj comes fully into consciousness. From 1876, after the end of the Mughal Empire and the dissolution of the East India Company, Queen Victoria carried the title "Empress of India". The allusion is made even more explicit when the word "empire", with its enjambment emphasis, appears in the next line. It seems as if the image of the Queen Empress is being projected backwards, distorting the idyll of the former stanza. The mechanisms of power are alien to the grandmother and she had to learn them from "the practised hands" of the colonizers. Now, instead of "delegating domestic chores", she is "tam[ing] the peacocks in the garden".

Up to the last line of the second stanza, the process of memory mainly takes place in the inner space of a world of objects, whereas the third stanza begins to extend the poem's spatial and historical dimension. The "city of merchant ships and parade-ground strife" referred to in the fourth stanza is the colonial port city of Madras (now Chennai), one of the most important commercial centers ("cartloads of spices plucked for colder ports") and military bases during the British Raj and the scene of numerous violent conflicts between nationalists and the British ("parade-ground strife"). The "rain-gashed heart / of that world" is also a metaphor for Madras, well known for its extreme monsoon rainfall. According to Brôcan (in *Die Ankunft der Vögel*), the actual biography of Hoskoté's grandmother shines through in the following lines:

> Like the poets of that city, she wrote in two languages,
> spoke a third in polite company, the lines enjambed
> over the trellises, the words trapped in porous stone.

The three languages that she spoke were Konkani, as her native tongue, Kannada, which is spoken in the Mangalore region where she spent her childhood, and, of course, English, spoken in "polite company". Therefore, it is this linguistic and cultural hybridity which forms a poetic multilingualism in which the "trellises" of language are "enjambed". However, this cannot be understood without taking into account the cultural and social language ideologies at work in the grandmother's (the poet's) choice of this or that particular code, reflecting pre-existing relationships of power: the words are still trapped in stone. Yet the stone is porous. Every language gives a different view on the world, which is mirrored and reflected back by other languages through the spoken and written word. It is this process of translation that challenges the unitary notion of a dominant language of power and nationhood, making the stone porous and vulnerable to erosion. The concept of the third space becomes explicit in the poem, in which new utterance and new forms of utterance are created. In the context of Hoskoté's writing, the line can also be read as an enabling gesture of writing.

In the next stanza, we witness the death of the grandmother, out of which emerges an imagery of death and rebirth.

> She died giving birth to a daughter
> on Armistice Day, 1931.
> She grew into the earth, then, a storied fig tree
> whose roots shot to heaven and branches burrowed
> so deep they seeded a forest.

The image of the "fig tree" with its roots above and branches below can be found in the *Upanishads* as well as the *Bhagavad-Gītā*. In the latter, the universe "is represented as a tree the roots of which are in heaven with branches stretching downward into the world" (James 1967, 148). The fig tree in the poem is likely to be an Asvatha tree from the *Bhagavad-Gītā*, which is a symbol of creation but also stands for "rebirth and the world of sense" (*ibid.*). The repetition of two syntagmas "[s]he died" and "[s]he grew" in lines 32 and 34 emphasizes the notion of rebirth by showing the process of dying and growing as mutually reinforcing. As its branches may seed a whole forest, the grandmother's figurative motherliness is elevated to such extent that she finally becomes a religious symbol herself, "a storied fig tree". This spiritual form of remembering is juxtaposed against Armistice Day, which commemorates those members of the armed forces who were killed during the First World War and which is named after the signing of the armistice between the Allies and Germany in 1918. Through her symbolic superelevation, the event of the grandmother's death eludes the historical narrative of the colonial power.

However, her turning into a symbol should not be hastily misread as a secret longing for Bharat Mata (Mother India), the national personification of India as a mother goddess, an image that evolved out of the Indian movement for independence and which even today is exploited by Hindu nationalists (McKean 1996). The grandmother was consumed by her giving, and so is the symbolic figure of the mother goddess. Now, the self wonders what this image of his grandmother still means to him in his present life circumstances, as the two are connected "by nothing more substantial / than a spiralled thread of protein". Although no longer *keeping a nostalgic* connection to what has been, he still wants to stay in contact with the deceased, to find out what potential future she was buried with. Forgetting her would simply be an act of repression. She appears to him at night, but her image is cut by the incoming light from the street. Again, we find that uncanny state of being-in-the-dark out of which the process of remembering is initiated.

In the poem's final stanza, the grandmother appears as a manifestation of her spirit in human form: the process of remembering is haunted by its subject. At last the person to whom the poem is dedicated and whose life is remembered speaks out herself. After line 43, the self switches to a listening position. The whole stanza is dominated by the grandmother's ghost's asking and appealing to her "son", saying that he should "hoard" his "powers" and "not give / from the core", emphasized by the epistrophe in lines 43 and 44. Giving "consumes", "spites" and "kills". He should not, like the hero Karna, practice a form of selfless generosity. Karna is a warrior from the traditional Indian Sanskrit epic *Mahābhārata*, who was born with golden armour and earrings that made him invincible in battle. He swore an oath that he would fulfil a request from anyone who approached him when he was worshipping the Sun at midday. Indra, disguised as a beggar, took advantage of this and asked Karna for his armour and earrings. Karna gave in and therefore later died unprotected in the Great War between the Kauravas and Pandavas (*Mahābhārata*, 147-49; 265-74). Karna is still a greatly admired role model within the Hindu community, especially because of his generous behavior towards others.

In the poem, there are two things that kill: the word "empress", and selfless giving. Colonial rule, her own life as well as the feudal-patriarchal Indian tradition have "consumed" the grandmother of the remembering self—a notion that is, as shown, evoked right from the first stanza through the ambiguous play with the metaphors of bodily memory. For the poem's literary consciousness, memories are not in the past, but live on as present realities to be both experienced and re-imagined, while at the same time reflecting that process and its medium. In "A Poem for Grandmother", remembering is evoked as moments of passage and transfer. In the context of cultural hybridity's images of memory, the lyrical genre has a special role, as it creates poetic images, which abjure traditional semantic patterns. These are vital signs of being-in-the-world. According to Brôcan, it is this state of "being-in-the-world" in the face of mortality which underlies Hoskoté's numerous dedication poems (103).

In the course of this essay, I have quoted several times from Jürgen Brôcan's generally excellent Afterword to his German translation of Hoskoté. Nevertheless, it is astonishing to see that he denies any element of nostalgia in Hoskoté's poetry, even though Hoskoté once confessed (in an interview with Clark Blaise, 1995) that "it's very strange to have nostalgia for a time before you were born". Homelessness, *i.e.*, constantly re-imagining the notion of home, might be a very productive state for an artist, but not necessarily a pleasant one. This feeling of nostalgia can be understood as a point of departure for his (2000b) identity-giving concept of spiritual homelessness "by which a spiritual homeland is re-created to replace a lost geographical or psychological homeland" (104).

As writer and cultural theorist, it is this spiritual aspect that distinguishes him from what he called, in *The Periphery and its Avatars: A Response to Documenta 11*, "the creative hybridity celebrated in Bhabhaist lore" (14). The aesthetic project of re-imagining the notion of home is related to an ethical one, which explores the given conditions of cultural encounters, asking how "to intervene in a world of objects with sensitivity, while not forgetting the world of the creators who made those objects" (Hoskoté 1998).

Such a sensitive intervention is different from the "conquistador model of love" that Hoskoté finds symbolized in Apollo's obsessive desire for Daphne in the Greek myth of Apollo and Daphne. In opposition to this stands a "sacred inviolability" between Self and Other which enables "an interplay between the ethical project and the aesthetic project, in which each becomes a possible source of values for the other" (*ibid.*). Hoskoté also takes up this subject in his poem "Apollo and Daphne" (2001), in which the reading of Apollo's "savage possession of the fleeing Other" as a classical pattern of desire is subverted through a shift of perspective. The poem observes Bernini's famous marble statue of Apollo and Daphne, stating that in its narrative movement the "chase remains in suspense", and Apollo's fingers freeze an "inch from [Daphne's] hair." Thus, "the sculptor preserves the rough suitor's shock" and "the terror of the unwilling bride". The act of possession is not fulfilled. Again, the poem here, as in "A Poem for Grandmother", becomes a place in which the ethical and aesthetic intertwine. Hoskoté's concept of "sacred inviolability" between Self and Other resembles the notion of the Buddhist metaphor of Indra's net, which is composed of an infinite number of jewels. Each of the jewels reflected in one jewel is also reflected in all the other jewels strung together in an infinite process of reflection (Cook 1981, 2). This symbolizes what Hoskoté sees to be "the defining condition for all post-colonial art, certainly for contemporary Indian art": "mutability" (Hoskoté 1998). The loss of a "consistent sense of self" establishes an "emancipatory condition" (*ibid.*) of renewal.

References

Andersen, Wayne. *Freud, Leonardo da Vinci and the Vulture's Tail: A Refreshing Look at Leonardo's Sexuality.* New York: Other Press, 2001.

Assmann, Aleida. "Zur Metaphorik der Erinnerung." In: *Mnemosyne: Formen und Funktionen der kulturellen Erinnerung.* Ed. Aleida Assmann / Dietrich Harth. Frankfurt/M.: Fischer Wissenschaft, 1991, 13-35.

------------ . *Erinnerungsräume: Formen und Wandlungen des kulturellen Gedächtnisses.* Munich: C. H: Beck, 1999.

Assmann, Jan. "Die Lebenden und die Toten." In: *Der Abschied von den Toten: Trauerrituale im Kulturvergleich.* Ed. Jan Assmann / Franz Maciejewski / Axel Michaels. Göttingen: Wallstein, 2005, 16-36.

------------ / Czaplicka, John. "Collective Memory and Cultural Identity." In: *New German Critique*, 65, Spring-Summer 1995, 125-33.

Bhabha, Homi K. *The Location of Culture* (1994). Oxford: Routledge Classics, 2005.

Borges, Jorge Luis. "A Poet's Creed." (1967). In: Jorge Luis Borges. *This Craft of Verse.* Cambridge, MA: Harvard University Press, 2000, 97-125.

Butzer, Günter. "Gedächtnismetaphorik." In: *Gedächtniskonzepte der Literaturwissenschaft: Theoretische Grundlegung und Anwendungsperspektiven.* Ed. Astrid Erll / Ansgar Nünning. Berlin: Walter De Gruyter, 2005, 11-29.

Cook, Francis H. *Hua-yen Buddhism: The Jewel Net of Indra* (1973). University Park, PA: Pennsylvania State University Press, 1981.

Erndl, Kathleen M. *Victory to the Mother: The Hindu Goddess of Northwest India in Myth, Ritual and Symbol.* Oxford: Oxford University Press, 1993.

Foucault, Michel. *The Archeology of Knowledge* [*L'Archéologie du Savoir*, 1969]. Transl. A. M. Sheridan Smith. London: Routledge. 2002.

Freud, Sigmund. *Leonardo da Vinci and a Memory of His Childhood* (*Eine Kindheitserinnerung des Leonardo da Vinci*, 1910). Transl. Alan Tyson. New York: W. W. Norton, 1961.

Heinz, Rudolf / Weismüller, Christoph. *Nachtgänge: Zur Philosophie des Somnambulismus*. Vienna: Passagen, 1996.

Hoskoté, Ranjit. *Zones of Assault*. New Delhi & Calcutta: Rupa & Co., 1991.

------------. "Interview with Clark Blaise of the University of Iowa" (1995). In: *Brisbane Blog*. Website, <http://brisbaneblog. info/2010/02/brisbane-art-discussions-ranjit-hoskote/>

------------ . "Beyond the House of Wonders: Some Remarks on the Possibility of Inter-cultural Communication." In: *Resartis*. Sixth General Meeting, 1998. Website, <No longer online>

------------ . *The Cartographer's Apprentice*. Bombay: Pundole Art Gallery, 2000a.

------------ / Dehejia, Harsha V. / Jha Shankar, Prem. *Despair and Modernity: Reflections from Modern Indian Painting*. Delhi: Motatil Banarsidass, 2000b.

------------ . *The Sleepwalker's Archive*. Bombay: Single File, 2001.

------------ (Ed.). *Reasons for Belonging: Fourteen Contemporary Indian Poets*. New Delhi: Penguin, 2002.

------------ . "The Periphery and its Avatars: A Response to Documenta 11." In: *Art and Thought: Goethe Institute Inter Nations*, 76, 1, October 2002-March 2003, 11-14.

------------ . *Vanishing Acts: New and Selected Poems 1985-2005*. New Delhi: Penguin, 2006a.

------------ . *Die Ankunft der Vögel: Gedichte*. Ed. and transl. Jürgen Brôcan. Munich: Carl Hanser, 2006b.

Humphrey, Richard. "Literarische Gattung und Gedächtnis." In: *Gedächtniskonzepte der Literaturwissenschaft: Theoretische Grundlegung und Anwendungsperspektiven*. Ed. Astrid Erll / Ansgar Nünning. Berlin: Walter De Gruyter, 2005, 73-96.

James, E. O. *The Tree of Life: An Archaeological Study*. Leiden: E. J. Brill, 1966.

Mahābhārata, Das: Ein altindisches Epos (1961). Ed. &

transl. Biren Roy (Sanskrit to English) and Elisabeth Roemer (into German). Düsseldorf: Eugen Diederichs, 1973.

Matt, Gerald / Fitz, Angelika / Wörgötter, Michael (Eds.). *Kapital & Karma: Aktuelle Positionen indischer Kunst*. Vienna: Kunsthalle, 2002.

McKean, Lise. *Divine Enterprise: Gurus and the Hindu Nationalist Movement*. Chicago: University of Chicago Press, 1996.

Neumann, Birgit. "The Literary Representation of Memory." In: *Cultural Memory Studies: An International and Interdisciplinary Handbook*. Ed. Astrid Erll / Ansgar Nünning / Sara B. Young. Berlin: Walter de Gruyter, 2008, 333-44.

Nünning, Ansgar (Ed.). *Metzler Lexikon Literatur- und Kulturtheorie: Ansätze—Personen—Grundbegriffe*. Third edition. Stuttgart: J. B. Metzler, 2004.

Patke, Rajeev S. *Postcolonial Poetry in English*. Oxford: Oxford University Press, 2006.

Rifkin, Libbie. *Career Moves: Olson, Creeley, Zukofsky, Berrigan, and the American Avant-Garde*. Madison, WI: University of Wisconsin Press, 2000.

Rutherford, Jonathan. "The Third Space: Interview with Homi Bhabha." In: *Identity: Community, Culture, Difference*. Ed. Jonathan Rutherford. London: Lawrence & Wishart, 1990, 207-21.

Subramaniam, Arundhathi. "Spy, Interpreter, Double Agent: Interview with Ranjit Hoskoté." In: *India—Poetry International Web*, June 1st, 2005. Website, <http://india.poetryinternationalweb.org/piw_cms/cms/cms_module/index.php?obj_id=2692>

Trojanow, Ilija. "Das Archiv des Schlafwandlers: Ilija Trojanow zu Ranjit Hoskoté." In: *Edition Lyrik Kabinett bei Hanser*. Website, <http://specials.hanser.de/lyrikkabinett/hoskote/index.asp?task=5>

Vries, Ad de. *Dictionary of Symbols and Imagery* (1973). Amsterdam: North-Holland Publishing Company, 1976.

Walsh, William. *Indian Literature in English*. London: Longman, 1990.

Weinrich, Harald. "Typen der Gedächtnismetaphorik." In: *Archiv für Begriffsgeschichte,* 9 (1964), 23-26.

SCOTLAND AND QUÉBEC

CULTURE AND IDENTITY
IN DRAMATIC TRANSLATION
BY MIRREN AUGUSTIN

PERSONAL IDENTITY, everyone will agree, is developed in a constant process of contrasting and comparing images of the self with those of others. National and cultural identities are formed through a similar process of demarcation or association on wider levels. Frequently, other cultures and nations—perceived through images, information, discourses, texts or institutions— represent a mirror with whose help the culture that receives their reflection can define itself. That may happen by opposing the Other, or by identifying with it. Relations between Scotland (a part of Britain) and Quebec (a part of Canada) provide an example of the latter. These two "stateless nations" (McCrone 1992) have spent the past fifty years reviewing the basis of their national identities with a view to achieving political and economic sovereignty. They have been the frequent subjects of comparisons, their perceived similarities offering comfort and inspiration.

This article illustrates where those comparisons were made, focussing on literary translation and, at the same time, language in general, both of which have been involved in the process of making exchanges possible and both of which are themselves much-discussed issues of identity. A particular emphasis is placed on the medium of the theater, which forms the mainstay of literary translations between the two, and which provides a useful basis for discussing major cultural motifs and their transformation (in continuation of the work carried out by Ian Lockerbie 1988, 2005, and Martin Bowman 1988, 2003, both of whom did much to help me when I was researching the material used in this article).

Before expanding on the topic, however, let me begin with a comparative overview of the two nations' political, social and cultural preoccupations.

Political Parallels

THE DISCUSSIONS in Scotland and Quebec regarding sovereignty have been very similar since the Seventies, when they became central to the political discourse of both nations. The transfer or exchange of practical knowledge and opinions was ongoing from 1975, when Parti Québécois leader René Lévesque stated on a visit to Scotland:

> I notice the same feeling here and the same kind of dismay about the central government system. [...] You can feel that Scotland is very much aware of a separate identity but is also becoming more frustrated. In that way we are very *sympathique* [*sic*] (quoted in Faux 1975).

He went on to say that Quebecers, however, were further along the line in terms of claiming full sovereignty. (It must be borne in mind that they already belonged to a federal system that was instituted with the Canadian Constitution Act of 1867, whereas there was no such kind of devolution yet in Scotland.) Furthermore, their political claims were accompanied by the actual social and cultural transformations of the Silent Revolution, begun in 1960, instigating changes in the welfare state and economic development and the cultural and linguistic protection of French Quebecers.

Only one year apart, both nations—the word used in

Anderson's sense of "imagined communities" (1989)—suffered similarly disappointing referendums on further independence (Scotland in 1979, Quebec in 1980) that led to the setback of the independent cause for the next decade. In Quebec, the second referendum in 1995 was equally unsuccessful; no new referendum is in sight. In Scotland, devolution was publicly voted for in 1997. Around 1998, with the creation of the Scotland Act that instituted a Scottish parliament, comparisons between the two nations intensified again, as Quebec, along with Catalonia, still appeared as a viable role model in terms of regional government and promotion of its separate culture. This is not to say that the manner of influence has been one-sided, since Quebec has always looked to Scotland because of its broad recognition as a nation, something Quebec itself did not officially receive from the Canadian government until 2006.

Cultural Parallels

POLITICAL SOVEREIGNTY is just one area in which discussions of national and cultural identity run along parallel lines. Affinities between Scotland and Quebec can be observed in three central areas of cultural singularity which have recurrently made up the traditional discourse of difference from their bigger neighbor: language, religion (more precisely, a particular relationship with religious authority that has informed society) and rural rootedness. Since language will be discussed later, let me first concentrate on religion and what can also be described as a parochial focus. They may have validated the expression of a distinct culture and ensured its survival, but they also contributed, as will be seen, to a collective memory that has many connotations of regression. Further, the difficulties surrounding the preservation of core values repeatedly lead to alienation or cultural insecurity. To make this point, let me summarize some key historical factors.

French Canadians, from their defeat on the Plains of Abraham (1759) and the Treaty of Paris (1763) on, when French

Canada was handed over to the British, were largely marginalized within the colonial economy and effectively subordinated by anglophone Canada despite retaining their own distinct institutions and systems in the areas of language, law, the church, and land tenure. The response to the danger of assimilation was a resistance that drew strength from the Roman Catholic faith and the pointed upkeep of French traditions in particular. The Catholic Church exerted a very strong influence on French Canadian society until the early twentieth century, contributing to a largely homogeneous, self-contained and distinct French Canadian culture—some interpenetration with Irish and Scottish cultural practices notwithstanding— but also keeping it fixed in its place and in poverty, not least through an extraordinarily high birth rate and few chances of further education. Linguistic and cultural survival were thereby assured within their class limits, but lack of economic opportunity and lack of social mobility in an increasingly urbanized society led to a build-up of frustration. Survival had come at the expense of evolution. The frustration was further fuelled by events such as the enforced conscription during both World Wars and the sudden economic rush after 1945, when the financial center of Canada moved from Montreal to Toronto, and ultimately released with the advent of the Silent Revolution in the Sixties. An ideology of "catching up" replaced that of conservatism and survival. The new dynamism and energy of French Quebecers of this time mark their "new" identity, yet it is consistently undercut by a collective memory which remains tied to a pre-industrial, parochial past, an image dominated by English Canadian oppression, but also religious containment and ethnic self-isolation. How to overcome or transform this frame of reference for a markedly ethnic Quebecois identity has been an open challenge for the past thirty years.

Concerning Scotland, although nationalists would tend to liken the relationship of the English and the Scots to that between English and French Canadians, the Union of 1707 was voluntary and by no means a conquest. The Lowlands and the urban centers profited from the union with England. Trade relations were facilitated. Glasgow built on its trade to the Americas to eventually become the Empire's second largest port, and Edinburgh flourished economically and intellectually as the "Athens of the North" in the Century of Enlightenment. Despite the fascination with the likes of Walter Scott's depictions, in his historical novels and narrative poems, of the failed Jacobite rebellions against the English monarchy, the general self-perception of Scots was that they were also Northern British. Only in the early twentieth century did the loyalty to Britain and the Empire wane, motivated by the increasingly unequal developments in England and Scotland and the lack of recognition of Scottish needs and interests, especially in terms of economic and planning policy. Before the Nineties, nationalist movements were particularly strong during the post-war disillusionment of the Twenties, surrounding the central issues of insufficient improvement of housing and working conditions, and in the Seventies, when oil was discovered off the coast of Scotland and economic autonomy appeared viable and even advisable.

From the Scottish Reformation in 1560 up until the twentieth century, Scottish culture had been marked deeply by the Calvinist faith, with its doctrine of predestination, creating a considerable contrast with the progressive thought developing among intellectuals from the eighteenth century onwards. Robert Louis Stevenson's *The Strange Case of Dr. Jekyll and Mr. Hyde*, a reflection of his own "Calvino-Agnosticism" and the moral dilemma resulting from it, is prescient of a myth that would occupy Scottish critics of the twentieth century for a long time. It is that of the split character of Scots, supposedly the reflection of contrasts and contradictions that are inherent within the Scottish mind and character. Under the term "Caledonian Antisyzygy" (introduced by Gregory Smith in 1919), it has come to encompass many things. Stemming from a forbidding, disenfranchizing religion on the one hand and the effects of anglicization on the other, Lockerbie considers cultural schizophrenia, guilt and alienation as some of the features which form an essential parallel with Quebec (1988, 9).

The dominant cultural clichés of Scottishness, surrounding Tartanry (the sentimentalized response to Scott's "cultural creation of the Highlands" as a viable symbol for the Scottish imaginary) and the related Kailyard (a literary school celebrating rural nostalgia and centered on a narrative of preserving parochial values), are pervasive wherever one looks (see Corbett 1997, 185 f.). At times when feelings of nationalism were at their strongest, they were usually rejected most strongly, in favor of urban and modern representations. This reflects the shift in focus, from the rural to the urban, in Quebec. However, urban representations too have become regressive, mostly because of a concentration on dominantly masculine, working-class and frequently violent images. Nonetheless, both continue to compete for representation and still exert an essential influence on discussions of cultural stereotypes and identities, even if much of it is ironic.

Language as a Central Feature in the Expression of Identity

IT IS at the confrontation of rural and urban identities that I wish to introduce in more detail the subject of language. More precisely, I will talk about vernacular language as the next marker of a specific culture and symbolic "container" of collective memory—and also the primary issue to set the Scottish-Quebecois literary exchange in motion.

There are not just one but *two* representations of the vernacular as a symbol for the nation which must be taken into account. Bowman describes the representation of *rural* Scots as "the vessel of the imagination" and *urban* Scots as that of "the loss of this imagination" (2003, 44), because of the frequent uprooting which urbanization incurred. As has been said, the ideological and referential frame shifted in both cases from the first (rural, pre-industrial nostalgia) to the second (working-class, predominantly male "heroism" and defeat), before moving on to other, more diverse interpretations.

A desire to achieve this third step is what lay at the root of the translators' impulse to translate the Quebecois play *Les Belles-Soeurs* into urban Scots: They wished to show that Scots had creative potential as a multi-voiced literary language (see Findlay 1980, 5). This was part of an ideologically motivated process of re-evaluating the importance of a distinct language and positively affirming a distinctive cultural and national identity.

From a linguistic perspective, they consistently emphasized the variety of registers used by the playwright Michel Tremblay that underlined the multi-facetedness of non-standard playwriting, and spoke out against the opinion that the language could convey only depressing, working-class realism. However, it must be taken into account that this is also how it was first perceived in Quebec, revealing an attitude to their own language that struck a chord with Scottish audiences.

In Quebec in 1968, *Les Belles-Soeurs* sparked the debate surrounding the French language in Canada in an essential way. On the surface, it is about a group of Montreal working-class women, sisters, sisters-in-law, neighbors, who meet in Germaine Lauzon's kitchen ostensibly to help her stick the stamps she has won in a company competition into booklets, with which she will be able to buy the company's goods to refurbish her home. As they stick, they chat about day-to-day matters in their families' lives, but the situation becomes increasingly tense as individuals' secrets are unveiled, and ends in mayhem when it becomes clear that most of them are surreptitiously letting the completed booklets vanish into their own pockets. Desperately funny at times, the seemingly mundane scene actually has the scope of a tragedy, underlined by structural elements such as the choir the ladies form to punctuate the narrative—but these aspects were not important in the critical discussion of the play until somewhat later. With the play being written entirely in *Joual*, the urban working-class language that had been "deformed" and "defaced" by contact with English and was seen as archaic, vulgar, incorrect and incomprehensible, the language issue was reviewed by many in a very negative manner. *Joual*—and the fact that it was being used on stage—was taken as a symbol of the degradation of the French language and, by extension, French culture. It supplied an argument in the fight to purify French and to resist any further "contamination" by English influences, as part of the Silent Revolution. Another aspect was to underline the "national alienation" of being caught somewhere between standard metropolitan French and English, that it evoked (Bouchard 1998, 230; Biron *et al.* 2007, 456).

Soon, however, the vernacular came to be used in the opposite way—more in the way in which Tremblay understood it—as an affirmative, political rewriting of what it meant to be a French Canadian. At the same time, theater became the "haut lieu" of identity affirmation, where the widespread use of *Joual* had nationalist connotations (Ladouceur 2005, 34). But use of the language was quickly identified as having limitations, serving mainly as a means of protest or to denounce a history of colonization and failure (Bouchard, 243 f.) It must be said that the need to confirm the normality of French in Quebec (as opposed to *Joual*) now informs the discourse of self-affirmation instead (Lockerbie 2005, 243), widening the gap between oral expression and written standards in literature again.

The word *Joual* continues to live on in the collective consciousness primarily as expressing the alienation of the past. What distinguishes it from regional dialects or sociolects (for today it is considered to be neither of these) is its "extension [...] from the realm of the local and the everyday into that of the symbolic and the *imaginaire*" (Lockerbie 2005, 231), meaning that it still stands as a symbol for the nation, much in the way that Scots (similarly hard to identify due to its many variations) does for Scotland.

Use of Scots and Scots-English dialects did become fashionable in literature around 1989—quite possibly with the help of Bowman and Findlay's translations—the year that *The Guid Sisters* (Scots translation of *Les Belles-Soeurs*) was finally staged after the script had lain gathering dust on producers' desks for almost a decade. It flourished in the political context of increasing nationalism, as a marker of difference from the English norm or standard. In the absence of a standardized spelling, authors who intended to reproduce spoken language frequently did so by over-emphasizing its graphemic distance from English. Corbett asserts that the "linguistic code of the nation [became] an icon of Scottishness" (1997, 9), one of continued cultural resistance to imposed norms. In being a popular medium of writing, it has come very close to what the translators originally intended, and—though that can only be speculated upon—theater authors may have received some inspiration from Tremblay's singular use of theatrical language into the bargain.

On the Meaning of Translation

Since I am speaking of the use of the vernacular as an icon of cultural resistance, then it must be emphasized that translation into vernacular or non-standard languages also constitutes a form of resistance, in particular to the assumption that through domestication—the preferred strategy of English-language translation, which pays little attention to the process and underlying meaning of translating—cultural differences can be eradicated and discourses unified (see Venuti 1995).

When looking at the meaning of translation in Scotland and Quebec it is therefore important to take into account the relationship that both have with their most direct and influential neighbor: in the one case, England, in the other, English-speaking Canada. Any translation that has an objective beyond simply making texts available in another language can be expected to deal with the problems that arise from this association or opposition.

In Quebec, the constant need to translate at institutional levels, lengthy and impractical, led to a hostile view of translation. With English the source—and thereby the indifferent authority—and French the perpetual target language, relations in everyday communication were basically fixed; the only way of circumventing them was by assimilating to English. Accordingly, writes Ladouceur, translation is traditionally "perceived as a symbol of political domination and an agent of linguistic assimilation" (34, my translation), and has come to stand as a metaphor for the alienation of French Canadians. However, literary translation is quite another matter, as shall be seen.

In Scotland, albeit excluding the question of Gaelic, it has been a long time since there was any need for translation. Scots and English have grown together, with Scots popularly being perceived as little more than a dialect or an accent of English. However, *theatrical* translation into Scots looks back on a history of half a millennium and has been revived in the past seventy years with the renewed purpose of "mark[ing] some degree of cultural independence, usually in implicit or explicit opposition to England and English" (Corbett 1999, 6 f.). Two things are at issue: the act of translating and appropriating as a form of opposition, resistance, or however you might like to call it, and the act of putting the language to literary use. As Findlay (2004) remarks:

> Reasons commonly given are that translation into Scots extends the capacities of the medium in meeting the challenge of a foreign-language work and that the status of Scots, through its association with the prestige work translated, is enhanced (6).

This ideological argument was also understood in Quebec, where translations into vernacular Quebecois French bloomed in the Seventies and Eighties, during the short phase of linguistic "identity affirmation". Brisset (1990) speaks of "identity translation" (*traduction identitaire*) to qualify the strategy of appropriating a lot of classic material and giving it a distinctly local flavor mainly through the use of marked *Joual*. Controversially, she points out to what extent theater translation in this era served its purpose of elevating the principles of a strongly rooted Quebecois culture and—once a proper tradition of playwriting had been established—quickly and happily faded out. (*Joual* also faded out to be replaced by the exploration of new possibilities of expression: It marked a turn to physical theater for some and a different kind of respect for language for others. Gaboriau has characterized the linguistic consciousness of text-based French Canadian drama as its constant "invisible character" (1995, 87), explaining that its connection to cultural survival and solidarity has resulted in a linguistic exuberance onstage that is, for example, very far from the English Canadian theater tradition. Instead, it shares much with Scottish drama, where audiences understand the language's ideological charge and generally hold linguistic expressiveness and wit in particularly high esteem.)

To sum up, translation of this kind in the early stages of the development of a proper, "national" literature may be regarded in the context of an anti-hegemonic cultural demarcation. Its meanings are at least threefold: First, to question and subvert dominant discourses of standardization and homogenization. Second, to enhance the powers of the language, which functions as a carrier of identity. Third, to serve as creative inspiration.

Where many translations originally consisted of relocations and appropriations, new translations that have a more source-oriented approach still have a validating effect for the target language and (theater) culture. As Findlay says in his *History of Scottish Theatre* (1998): "Through translation, theatre production in Scotland [can] be seen as part of an international cultural ecology, or as a branch management of a global business" (305). Neither the source nor the target necessarily loses its imprint. And so, in various ways, translations continue to position universal issues in the local and vice versa.

It is with one (more) facet of this final observation that I'd like to conclude, by giving some examples of the subjects that were highlighted as communicating experiences shared between Scots and Quebecers. They will no doubt find their equivalents elsewhere in global experiences of the late twentieth century, but the connotations—discussed as national issues—are so close, I would contend, that they might almost coincide.

In the case of *Les Belles-Soeurs'* reception, Glasgow's working-class—a very familiar subject in Scottish literature—was discovered to have "what seemed like a long-lost twin across the Atlantic" (McMillan 2000). On a more universal level, Tremblay's play, as well as obviously addressing gender issues with an unprecedented cast of fifteen women, contained a critique of capitalism and consumerism; it exposed the falling apart of community structures to be replaced by people in search of personal freedom. On closer inspection, what the language and its speakers stood for was immediately recognizable from the discourse of the Seventies and Eighties. It encompassed an understanding of "linguistic fracture" and status losses, the losses endured through urbanization, extremely rapid social change that left many with a feeling of being marginalized, and what McMillan termed "unspoken cultural loss", somewhere in the sense that the elements that constituted a distinct culture (particularly religion and community) no longer mattered any more (McMillan 2000, as quoted by Bowman 2003, 41 f.).

A more recent example is that of the fast-paced comedy *Passing Places* (written by Stephen Greenhorn, 1997), which in turn was translated into Quebecois French (and staged in 2006). Its second title, "A road movie for the stage", under-lines a common fascination with the American film models and tropes surrounding the road trip and "going West". However, in this case the central characters, two bored young dropouts from Motherwell, the former capital of Scottish steel production, travel north in their quest to sell a stolen surfboard. In his intro-duction to the collection in which the play was printed, Philip Howard views it as, "in many ways, the ultimate Scotland Play" and the trip as "a classic Scottish journey", below which lies the pursuit of something—a sense of identity and belonging—to hold on to (1998, ix). The experience of de-industrialization and ensuing marginalization and social dependency in the post-

Thatcher years is shown as a major fracture, as a result of which young, urbanized people of their generation have grown up with a sense of dislocation. Scotland, in the boys' eyes, is perceived not in terms of "home", but as a postcard cliché. There can be no talk of a return to their roots, which—historically—have been severed. Their encounters en route are classic, with all sorts of colorful, anti-clichéd characters who make them question their identity and speak for an understanding of Scotland as a culturally diverse, universally connected country with a positive disposition towards the future. It reflects the re-definition of a more open and inclusive Scottishness in the context of devolution: re-branding Scotland. The reconnection with the cultural geography of the nation, transcendence of cultural insecurity and trivialization and the search for identity occur at the transition into nationhood, the situation in which Quebec finds itself—still.

In terms of content and time-line, *Les Belles-Soeurs* and *Passing Places* contrast very nicely, the one looking backward, the other forward, discursively reflecting the changes that have been achieved. *Passing Places* suggests a more progressive and positive tone on identity that *can* (note the use of the modal) be adopted. Once more, though explicitly this time, language is a subject in itself, in connection with the trope of alienation. Alex believes himself to be incapable of using the word "beautiful" to express his feelings along the way, because the concept is simply unknown to him. However, when they arrive at their destination and look out north over the sea, he wryly ends: "I'd like to be able to say 'beautiful' in Swedish" (226), suggesting that the journey (of self-discovery) is not yet over.

Conclusion

LITERARY TRANSLATION functions as the major facilitator of cultural exchange. It is not enough to see it as the simple process of making texts available in another language. More, it allows us to gain an insight into another culture while also recognizing ourselves through it, by drawing parallels and/or highlighting differences. In theater, the added factor is that the focus in directing is usually on the expectations of the recipients more than on the original text, and therefore is more likely to lead the audience to recognize "themselves" onstage. The immediacy and the communality of the experience are such that an actual effect going beyond the individual can also be felt and described by critics. See how McMillan describes the reception of *Les Belles-Soeurs*, for example:

> The crucial factor that made audiences sit up and take notice was that although all the characters spoke a rich vernacular Scots, they remained obviously rooted— by their names, their references, their culture—in the working-class east end of Montreal, where the play was conceived and written. At a stroke, all kinds of cultural barriers went crashing down.

Deviating from the usual procedure, I'd like to conclude on a personal note. I did not yet know about the Scottish-Quebecois connection when I saw the Quebecois production of *Passing Places* in 2006. But to experience its Montreal reception—the instant pleasure of the audience watching the characters hazardously drive through the Scottish mountains and blithely roll out Scottish place names in a rich French Canadian tongue—had precisely the same landslide effect on me. I identified at once with the culture it came from (which is half of my own) and connected with Quebecois audiences in the knowledge of being understood.

References

Anderson, Benedict. *Imagined Communities: Reflections on the Origin and Spread of Nationalism*. London: Verso, 1989.
Biron, Michel / Dumont, François / Nardout-Lafarge, Elisabeth. *Histoire de la littérature québécoise*. Montreal:

Boréal, 2007.

Bouchard, Chantal. *La langue et le nombril: Histoire d'une obsession québécoise*. Montreal: Fides, 1998.

Bowman, Martin. "*Joual* / Scots: The Language Issue in Michel Tremblay's *Les Belles-Soeurs*." In: Lockerbie (Ed.), 1988, 42-55.

------------. "Michel Tremblay in Scots: Celebration and Rehabilitation." In: *Performing National Identities: International Perspectives on Contemporary Canadian Theatre*. Ed. Grace Sherrill / Albert-Reiner Glaap. Vancouver: Talonbooks, 2003, 38-50.

Brisset, Annie. *Sociocritique de la traduction: Théâtre et altérité au Québec, 1968-1988*. Longueuil: Le Préambule, 1990.

Corbett, John. *Language and Scottish Literature*. Edinburgh: Edinburgh University Press, 1997.

------------. *Written in the Language of the Scottish Nation. A History of Literary Translation into Scots*. Clevedon: Multilingual Matters, 1999.

Faux, Ronald. "The Man from Quebec with a Message for Scotland." In: *The Times*, June 17th, 1985, 14.

Findlay, Bill. "Les Belles Soeurs (An Extract)." In: *Cencrastus*, 3, 1980, 4-8.

------------ (Ed.). *A History of Scottish Theatre*. Edinburgh: Polygon, 1998.

------------ (Ed.). *Frae Ither Tongues: Essays on Modern Translations into Scots*. Clevedon: Multilingual Matters, 2004.

Gaboriau, Linda. "The Cultures of Theatre." In: *Culture in Transit: Translating the Literature of Quebec*. Ed. Sherry Simon. Montreal: Véhicule Press, 1995, 83-90.

Greenhorn, Stephen (1997). "Passing Places." In: *Scotland Plays*. Ed. Philip Howard. London: Nick Hern, 1998, 137-226.

Ladouceur, Louise. *Making the Scene: La traduction du théâtre d'une langue officielle à l'autre au Canada*. Quebec: Éditions Nota bene, 2005.

Lockerbie, Ian. "Scotland and Quebec." In: *Image and Identity: Theatre and Cinema in Scotland and Quebec*. Ed. Ian

Lockerbie. Stirling: John Grierson Archive, 1988, 5-16.

------------. "The Place of Vernacular Languages in the Cultural Identities of Québec and Scotland." In: *British Journal of Canadian Studies*, 18, 2, 2005, 231-45.

McCrone, David. *Understanding Scotland: The Sociology of a Stateless Nation.* London: Routledge, 1992.

McMillan, Joyce. "A Languish in Language as Tremblay Traverses the Gap." In: *The Scotsman*, April 26th, 2000, 13.

Smith, G. Gregory (1919). *Scottish Literature: Character and Influence.* Reprint. Folcroft, PA: Folcroft Library Editions, 1972.

Venuti, Lawrence. *The Translator's Invisibility: A History of Translation.* London: Routledge, 1995.

THE DYNAMICS OF MYTH

LUIS VALDEZ'S *BERNABE* AND HAGGAG
ODDOUL'S *THE RIVER PEOPLE*
BY GHADA M. ABDEL HAFEEZ

MYTH, A SACRED NARRATIVE that once had religious significance shared by a group of people, reflects, as Anath Ariel De Vidas (2002) has put it, "indigenous thought by combining the amnesiac memory of the group with its cosmology and historical and social facts in order to explain the group's current situation" (209). In this sense, it is a kind of communal experience; a form of the repressed emotions of a community; its identity; and it operates by bringing the individual into a relationship with members of his cultural group on the basis of a certain cultural logic and common needs.

Cultural anthropologists and psychologists have long recognized that different geographical areas have unveiled remarkable parallels in the themes and plots of myths. The structural anthropologist Lévi-Strauss (1955), for example, argues that there is, indeed, "an astounding similarity between myths collected in widely different regions" (208). Carl Jung maintained that we all have a collective unconscious that unites us through universal "archetypes" (see Walker 2002). Joseph Campbell (1949) similarly claims that all cultures have a hero-quest-myth. They have given a positive impetus refocusing on myth; as they saw in it an invaluable source for defining the national, religious, and aesthetic essence of cultures and their inner identity.

When we study a myth, we are simultaneously studying difference and commonality. As Wendy Doniger (1998) says: "Myth is cross-culturally translatable, which is to say comparable, commensurable" (9). The external surface of a myth reflects the experience of a certain culture, but at a deeper level a common symbolic and archetypal "language" unifies the seemingly different myths. So, the cross-cultural comparison of myths is pragmatically possible, intellectually plausible, and politically productive (4 f.). Whether the hero of a myth is Indian, Chicano, or Nubian, this figure is on a universal quest for identity. David Adams Leeming highlights in his book *The World of Myth* (1992) that this essential similarity within different myths, irrespective of chronology and geography, indicates a collective authorship (7).

It is the purpose of this paper to compare the shared dynamics of myths in Luiz Valdez's play *Bernabe* (1986) and Haggag Hassan Oddoul's play *The River People* (1993) in addition to the two writers' critical dramatization of their respective ethnic identities. The two myths used are cultural versions of similar universal tendencies. Another premise of the paper is that such a comparison provides enlightening instances of the writers' reliance on both myth *and* landscape and myth *in* landscape. The paper also highlights the fusion and merging of self with the local topography, the nourishing earth, Mother Earth, La Tierra, in the first and with the Nile and the River People in the second.

What is meant when we say that the myths used in Valdez and Oddoul's plays are similar while acknowledging that the context is different? Context is an essential explanatory rubric to illuminate our understanding of the reasons behind comparing the myths used by these two particular writers. Jung saw myth as culturally elaborated "representations of situations" (quoted in Walker, 18). Chicanos and Nubians are two minority groups, misrepresented and underrepresented both in the arts and in other facets of life. They live on the fringes of their respective national societies. Both have been disenfranchised from their cultures and from their lands: Aztlan—an Indian name for a large area of the Southwest, predating the Spanish conquest of Mexico by centuries and redolent of both authenticity and loss (Catherine Wiley 1998)—and Nubia—an ancient land extending along the great legendary river, the Nile—which make up much of their landscape of the mind and of setting, are sacred places that determine who they are and what their writing is about. Like other marginalized groups, they endeavor to maintain their cultural identity by appropriating ethnographic essentialism to authenticate their own experience, as a form of creative resistance to the center (Spivak, in McRobbie 1985, 7). They articulate new consciousnesses that force the dominant to examine the contradictions. They have also reclaimed their cultural heritages, including mythology. Then they incorporate them as a means of being creative not only in communicating experiences different from those of the dominant, but also express their resistance to them. To achieve their goals, they investigate and draw their imagery and subject matter from their ancient myths; similarly, they take over their rhythm and style. The Aztec and Mayan myths and the Nubian have become inspirations for the philosophy and dramaturgy of Valdez and Oddoul. In creating their works, they try to find voices and forms that will speak against repression, racism, exclusion, and stereotypes. In their refusal to accept subordination, marginality, and the identity imposed upon them, both playwrights break down the shackles that have been put upon them; that imprison them in their inferior status.

Belonging to marginalized communities that have been threatened with radical effacement, both Luis Valdez (b. 1940)—a famous Chicano playwright, who founded the Teatro Campesino in the fields of Delano as a means of raising the political consciousness of the farmworkers—and Haggag Hassan Oddoul (b. 1944)—a renowned Nubian writer who was awarded the Egyptian State Prize for Short Stories in 1990—have recognized their own perspectives, concepts, ideologies, and interpretation of their cultures. For them, marginality has become a field of maneuver as they have seen themselves and all that they stood for as continually being regarded with disdain. Such a situation is not historically unique. It has been repeated many times with other minorities whose identity has been threatened. This situation has stimulated them to present their own version of grand narratives as countercanons to the national ones. To them, myth is neither a fictitious story, nor an interpretation of a dead past. Rather, it is an account of a reality which is larger than life. They rely on myth to explain the inexplicable, what some would call the supernatural. Myth, for them, constitutes a form of adaptation to reality and influences the crystalliza-tion of the individual identity and the formation of the superego. Using myth, moreover, reflects the writers' struggles with their marginality within their hostile environments. Living on the fringe of their national societies, they have to maintain their indigenous thought by combining local topography with their ancestral myths as well as establishing a homology between their culture, their people, and their terrain.

Both writers acknowledge the national aesthetic essence that myth plays in the development of the self-image that precedes nation-creation. In this way, they come close to Benedict Anderson (1983) who, in his important study on nation-building, defines "nation" as an "imagined community" because "the members of even the smallest nation will never know most of their fellow-members, meet them, or even hear them, yet in the minds of each lives the image of their communion" (112). Nation-building, Anderson asserts, is closely tied to print communities formed around newspapers and novels that nurture the precon-ceived notions that groups have of themselves as they wish to be, as they imagine themselves to be (30). Nations, then, adds Timothy Brennan (1991), "are imaginary constructs that depend for their existence on an apparatus in which imaginative litera-ture plays a decisive role" (49). Fully aware of this, the two play-wrights endeavor to instill the strong sense of their "imagined communities" through recovering, revising, and revisiting their myths. For them, the nation is, therefore, in the words of John

Hutchinson (1994),

> a collectivity of meaning, a bond "embedded in history" through common myths, symbols, narratives and other cultural forms, all of which enable "a people" to recognize itself as a commonality as opposed to others who do not have access to this fund of historical memories (xiii).

To mobilize their communities, Valdez and Oddoul instil a community sense of self-worth. They attempt to influence their communities' pride and nationalism through the elevation of their indigenous myth, memories, traditions—symbols of their ethnic heritages and the ways in which their living past has been, and can be, rediscovered and reinterpreted. In his interview with Roberto Orona-Cordova (1983), Valdez sees myth as "an underlying structure of a truth that is just below the surface of reality" (98). Oddoul, too, explains his deep faith in myth when he says:

> My use of legends only happens unconsciously. It has a lot to do with the fact that I come from a culture in which legends and myths are rife. The moment of ecstasy for me as a writer is when I sit down at my desk and feel that my ancestors are dictating their mysteries to me (quoted in Amin 2002, website)

Deeply rooted in their native folkways and regional landscapes, the two writers interweave myth into their narratives and strike a deep chord in portraying ways of relating to the earth. Both convey "archetypally" the symbolic nature of certain places and objects. Their beliefs embody a feeling of close association and affinity between Man and Earth, the mother, the nourisher, who is for both writers a muse and an inspiration. The Chicanos' spirituality is a land-based spirituality. The relationship between the land and the people is one of mystical inter-dependence. The Chicanos are of the land. Land or La Tierra is their life-cord in the same way as the Nile is for the Nubians. For the Nubians of the past, the Nile was worshiped just as Hapy, the bringer of fertility, was worshiped by ancient Egyptians. As one of their writers, Khalil Qasem (2006) has said: "The Nubians see God in the Nile and consequently love and fear him as they worship and dread God" (quoted in Oddoul, *Nubian Writers*, 2006, 68). For them, the Nile is their nourisher who gives generously but, when enraged, viciously devours their children and smashes their boats. That the two writers have different mythological expressions for the relationship between Man and Earth corresponds to the way in which each of them defines his relationship to the energy of the place according to their very culturally-specific world views. The external surface of the two myths reflects the unique experience of each culture but, at a deeper level, the Chicano and Nubian myths are unified by a common "archetypal" language.

David Adams Leeming suggests that in the modern literary or psychological sense, places and objects in myth are symbols and have "archetypal" significance (315), in which the question of spatial origins looms especially large. How does this association between the group and the terrain come about? Over time, the terrains in question are felt to provide the unique and indispensable setting for the events that shaped the community. Thus both La Tierra and the Nile, endowed by their people with properties of the sacred, have a connotative significance that transcends time and place. This reveals a set of human concerns that surpass any cultural barriers—experiences that we might call cross-cultural or transcultural.

In spite of the different geographical and historical circumstances that have shaped the two writers, there are striking parallels between *Bernabe* and *The River People* that may have resulted from recurrent reactions of the human psyche to similar situations or stimuli, *i.e.*, their land. Aztlan, defined by Gloria Anzaldua in her famous book *Borderlands / La Frontera* (1987) as "the land of herons, land of whiteness, the Edenic place of origin of Azteca" (26), and Nubia, the seat of one of the world's oldest civilizations and richest cultures, which make up much of their respective landscapes of mind and text, are sacred places for them that determine who they are. While the Chicanos' peregrination lasted two hundred years, and at the end of this journey they established themselves in the Valley of Mexico in the late twelfth century, the Nubians' habitation lasted until the Sixties of the last century; then the land was drowned by the building of the High Dam.

Both Valdez and Oddoul are haunted by their lost lands. Before the war with the United States that ended in 1848, Mexico possessed the Southwest. Chicanos consider themselves indigenous to the region. They rely on the anthropological findings that have proved that their ancestors explored and settled in parts of the Southwest not only as early as the sixteenth century but thousands of years earlier than that. The Chicanos are different from the Mexican nationals in the fact that they regard the Southwest rather than Mexico as their homeland; or, to be more exact, their lost homeland; the conquered northern half of the Mexican nation. Valdez, in an interesting comment, says: "We crossed no ocean [...] No Statue of Liberty ever greeted our arrival in this country [...] We did not, in fact, come to the United States at all. The United States came to us" (quoted in Broyles-Gonzales 2006, 276). After its defeat in 1848, Mexico ceded the region and its inhabitants to the United States. In spite of the guarantees in the Treaty of Guadalupe Hildalgo, the influx of white settlers combined with the history of violence and hatred in Southern Texas stripped millions of Indians and Mexicans of their lands. As a result, the Mexicans and Indians were both reduced to minority status. Since then, they have been imprisoned in the stereotype of the lazy, dirty, uneducated, and the sombrero-clad bandit.

The Nubian context is different and more insidious because the Nubians were forced by what Oddoul ("Nubian Literature", 2002) describes as "cosmic changes" (17) that took place in the twentieth century to leave their fertile lands, palm-trees, water wheels, and ancestral graveyards. The construction of the Aswan Dam in 1902 and then the High Dam in 1960, which Helen Miles (1994) has called the "death knell for the kingdom of Nubia", started the Nubians' exodus and Nubia, with its once sleepy backwater villages, was lost forever. Some of the Nubians resentfully accepted their life in the mountainous barren wilderness of Komombo while others migrated to larger cities like Alexandria. The resettlement in the arid desert in Upper Egypt or in the big cities did not make amends for what happened, as they all share the experience of dislodgement and denigration in their exile. This is the older generation's trauma, of course; because the younger generation of Nubians, who were born and grew up in the big cities, hardly understand their parents' "exile" culture, yet through their behavior they feel the differences which distinguish them from the rest of the Egyptians.

As in the case of the Chicanos, the Nubians have been victims of uncomplimentary references and stereotypic attitudes on the part of some of their numerically superior fellow citizens. Because Nubians speak a different language and practice different customs and traditions from their Egyptian and Sudanese neighbors, Nubia has become "a museum and folklore" and the Nubians have been relegated to the inferior status of janitors, waiters and cooks (Oddoul, *The Role of the Nubian Writer*, website, 2006).

Internalizing assumptions that Chicano and Nubian cultures differ from mainstream cultures, many Chicanos and Nubians—especially youth who come of age in school systems that preach assimilation at all costs—feel ashamed of their cultural roots. To make things worse, the new generations that have grown up in exile are taught very little, if anything at all, about their indigenous cultures other than the historically negative narratives. They do not use their native tongues either. As a result, our two writers respond to oppression by using the written word as a weapon against aggression and geographical displacement. Valdez—as Elizabeth Ramirez (1996) has pointed out—"stands out for his use of the drama to educate and inform others about

Chicano culture" (202). Oddoul (2006) similarly believes that every "true" Nubian has a role not only towards non-Nubians but also towards his own people. He has to save the Nubian identity from "being dispersed and consumed" (*About Nubia and Bahaa Taher*, website, 2006) by educating them that "they have a glorious past [...] and that their history and culture are not marginal" (*The Role of the Nubian Writer*, website, 2006).

Although, as Lavie / Swedenburg (1996) emphasize, the traumatic experiences of profound dislocation and displacement "[are] not experienced in precisely the same way across time and space, and [do] not unfold in a uniform fashion" (4), they have motivated the two writers to resist and reject the restrictive and all-encompassing social imagery and produce new forms of aesthetics, or counter-texts. Both writers have invested their ancient cultural pools and produced plays rich in spectacle, music, chanting, and bodies in motion. Valdez (1990) admits in *Early Works* that "Chicano theater must be revolutionary in technique as well as content" (6). The two plays differ in their stylistic qualities; while one favors the dream state and surrealistic images while the other is wrapped in romantic realism, both, however, present a different value scale from the dominant. Both, furthermore, promote the unconscious and the emotional side of human nature, aiming at restoring the natural relationship with the spiritual universe.

Similar recalling of their dispossession and of similar associations of man and nature, and life after death in nature, can be found in the two plays. The two playwrights create, in a complex and sophisticated way, a private and intimate universe, where lines between the past and the present are blurred and where those between life and death vanish. Everything from the past takes place simultaneously with the present. There is no death, but rather a continuous process of becoming, of growth, of deterioration and rebirth. In Valdez's play, his protagonist, the village idiot Bernabe, is in love with La Tierra, and in Oddoul's, his female protagonist, Asha Ashry, born the year the High Dam was built, is infatuated with the Nile and its people.

Both protagonists partake of the inspiring power of the landscape. *Bernabe* and *The River People* are thus explorations of man's relationship with the natural forces that God has endowed him with and which he dissipates by his arrogance and greed.

As the experiences vary, so do the products of the projective systems in myth. Valdez and Oddoul, breathing a new conscious literary life into their old myths, have found new ways to analyze their national and aesthetic essence suitable to their own cultures. The two plays present contemporary myths, whose characters inhabit conflicting temporalities; the external surfaces of the two plays reflect the experiences of the two cultures in question. *Bernabe*, based on the ritual of human sacrifice to Huitzilopochtli, the Aztec Sun God, is populated by El Sol, La Luna, and La Tierra. On the other hand, in *The River People*, which is also a mythical reinterpretation of the sacred relationship between the Nubians and the Nile, with remnants of folk traditions and the extinct worship of the Nile, we find the River People, mermaids, and perch. At a deeper level, the fact that at the end of the first play Bernabe eagerly sacrifices his heart to the Sun to prove his loyalty to La Tierra, while Asha drowns herself to become one of the River People, unifies them by a common "archetypal" language.

Bernabe was written in 1969, a year that witnessed a drastic change in Valdez's attitude towards Chicano theater: he deserted the agit-prop *actos* and moved towards what he calls as "a *teatro* of ritual, of music, of beauty and spiritual sensitivity. A *teatro* of legends and myths" ("Notes on Chicano Theatre", in *Early Works*, 9). He started integrating the Chicanos' cultural heritage with the *mito,* or myth form. He was motivated by the Chicanos' growing desire to investigate their roots in Pre-Columbian philosophy, science, religion, and art. Jorge Huerta (2000) explains that *mito* was Valdez's "response to philosophical Eurocentrism as well as realism in the theater" (37). Elizabeth Ramirez contends that Valdez used the *mito* because he felt it would help Chicanos rediscover their long-forgotten cultural heritage (193 f.). If the *actos* were created "through the eyes of man", the *mitos* were created "through the eyes of God" (Valdez, *Early Works*, 5). It is worth noting here that the "God" is not the Judeo-Christian deity but the Sun God, Huitzilopochtli. It is no surprise that his play is dominated by mythological figures that are used in a central way. In *Bernabe*, Valdez has endeavored to bring the gods back to their contemporary audiences. In his attempt to reveal some differences between Christian theology and indigenous beliefs, Valdez locates his play on several levels of material and mythical reality.

Bernabe is a "realistic fantasy" (Huerta, "The Influences of Latin American Theater on *Teatro Chicano*," 1983, 70), divided into seven scenes. It takes place in a rural town in the San Joaquin Valley of California where "the sun is lord and master" (*Bernabe*, 23). Valdez believes that everything is due to solar energy. In his article "A Return to Aztec and Mayan Roots" (1974), Theodore Shang explains Valdez's belief by saying that man eats plants and animals which have eaten plants and thereby consumes solar energy. He adds that within man and nature there is "conscious energy," which determines that a human embryo will develop into a human being. It also makes him want to become greater than he is in normal life by plugging into the conscious energy surrounding him. This requires him, according to Valdez, to be in harmony with other human beings and with nature lest he become brutal, violent, and cause psychic or physical harm to himself or others (62).

The first part of the play is a realistic portrayal of Bernabe's life with his mother in the *barrio*. The play's title character is a mentally-retarded farm worker in his early thirties, who is— as Valdez says in his introduction to the play—"touched with cosmic madness" (*Bernabe*, 23). From the very beginning of the play, we are confronted with two worlds: the world of man that Bernabe inhabits, and his own world. He is judged by the outside world as "insane but harmless" (*ibid.*). In his own world, which is "a world of profoundly elemental perceptions", Bernabe is a "human being living in direct relationship to earth, moon, sun, and stars" (*ibid.*). As Robert Hurwitt (1986) in his introduction to *Bernabe* explains: "There is a central duality in the character of Bernabe: there is divinity in madness." Bernabe can be regarded as the "archetypal" Chicano pursuing an eternal bond with Mother Earth, La Tierra.

Bernabe is the only son of a typical Catholic *madre*, who keeps on throughout the play warning him against sexual relations by emphasizing: "The ground [will] open up and swallow you. That's what happens to sons who don't respect their mothers. The earth opens up and swallows them *alive*" (*Bernabe*, in *Early Works*, 137). It is interesting to note that for the devout Catholic mother, who has probably been taught through Church narratives, the depths of the earth represent everlasting torment and punishment. For Bernabe, however, the depths of the earth represent the safety and warmth of Mother Earth's mythic womb. His regression to the idea of the mythic womb might be interpreted as a wish to flee from life and return to a fetal state or an unconscious wish for healthy adult love-making. Bernabe's belief in "Earth as Mother" comes as a contrast to the Judeo-Christian concept of God the Father. Through the worship of the fertility goddess, Bernabe creates a universe rich in life, freedom, and rebirth. The mother's warning foreshadows the major action of the play, as Bernabe will end up being swallowed by Mother Earth.

Poverty looms over the village. *Madre* hands Bernabe "preciously" a ten dollar bill to buy some basic items and refuses vehemently to allow him to buy an ice-cream. At the same time, she asks him to beg the labor contractor for work, reassuring him that his leg "is fine now" (137). If money is the axis around which the characters' lives rotate, Bernabe's revolves around his love for La Tierra; that is withering because it is running out of its natural resources. To him, the land should not belong to any person. It is not a property because it belongs to the community as a whole. It is Mother Earth which nurtures all people. That is what he confirms in the following exchange with Torres and Primo (139 f.):

BERNABE: I need money to buy la tierra.

TORRES: What tierra?

BERNABE: This one. Here and there and all over.

PRIMO *(humoring him)*: You wanna buy a ranchito?

BERNABE *(emphatically)*: No, a big rancho—with lots of tierra! All the tierra on earth. She's all mine.

TORRES: Yours?

BERNABE: My woman. We're gonna get married.

[...]

PRIMO *exits. Long pause.* BERNABE *kneels on the earth.*

BERNABE *(slyly)*: Tierra, they think I'm crazy. But you know I love you. *(Looks around)* See you tonight, eh?...like always. *(He kisses the ground and exits)*

To the normal characters, Bernabe's desire is indicative of his mental state, which encourages his male relatives—El Primo and El Tio—to set him up on a visit with Consuelo, the village prostitute, to distract him from the inescapable lure of La Tierra. It is here, in the prostitute's room, that the play shifts from realism to a dreamlike fantasy when we enter Bernabe's mind and see the workings of his distorted vision. Once he knows that he has been ensnared, he envisions his mother dressed in Consuelo's clothes and hears her reprimanding him for having sex. He is so tormented by guilt and panic that he repeats his mother's warnings that La Luna will swallow him, for being dirty (152). When the images of two women are blurred together in his mind, the effect is —as indicated in the stage directions—"nightmarish"

(155). He flees from the hotel thinking that he has killed his cousin, Torres, and hides in the hole that he dug in the ground where, as Tio says: "he crawls in and hides" (142). This hole is the mythic womb of La Tierra that makes him feel reborn again into nature's wholeness.

The play's last two scenes take us on a mythical journey, in which Bernabe is first visited by Luna (the moon) dressed as "a Pachuco, 1942-style: Zoot suit, drapes, calcos, hat with feather, small chain, *etc.*" (157), who arranges an assignation with his sister La Tierra (the earth), personified as "a soldadera [soldier woman of the Mexican Revolution, 1910] with a sombrero and cartridge belts" (158). La Tierra questions Bernabe's protestation of love: "Where and when have you stood up for me? All your life you've worked in the fields like a dog—and for what? So others can get rich on your sweat, while other men lay claim to me?" (160). She teaches him that true love means respecting her, fighting for her, and "being capable of killing those who have [her]" because as she says: "I was never meant to be the property of any man" (160). Jorge Huerta (1982) comments that this *soldadera*, this vision from the past who encompasses both an indigenous deity (La Tierra) and an archetypal heroine from recent history, is forcing Bernabe to show an independence and assertiveness that will make him whole (197). She is helping this "idiot" to emerge in rebirth from the womb of the earth into a new individuated existence, a new wisdom or wholeness, "como los machos". He begins to be transformed in front of our eyes when he admits to La Tierra's father, El Sol—who appears as the Aztec Sun God, Huitzilopochtli—that although he is described as "a loco", a madman, he knows that "the rich people are more locos than [him]" because, as he adds: "They sell la Tierra all the time, in little pedacitos here and there, but I know she should never be sold like that...because she doesn't belong to anyone" (*Bernabe*, in *Early Works*, 164). The one described as an idiot is the only one who is in harmony with nature. Both La Tierra and El Sol know his true nature, which has been hidden under the façade of craziness. La Tierra admits: "Since the very day of his birth, he has been innocent, and good. Others have laughed at him. But he has always come to my arms seeking warmth. He loves me with intensity most men cannot even imagine" (161). Her father also agrees that Bernabe is "the last of a great noble lineage of men I once knew in ancient times, and the first of a new raza cósmica that shall inherit the earth" (164). El Sol informs Bernabe that there were once men like him who respected La Tierra. "They saw what only a loco can understand," he reiterates, "that life is death and death is life" (*ibid.*). He now knows that death is the end point of one cycle and the beginning of another. This reflects his recognition of his active role in the maintenance of cosmic balance and the continuation of the existence of the universe.

In a dramatized representation that echoes the Aztec ceremonial sacrifices, Bernabe, god-impersonator, agrees to give his heart to El Sol so that he can continue to feed life.

Probing deeply into the religious Aztec vision of the cosmos, man was viewed as the collaborator of the gods, particularly of the sun, Huitzilopochtli. Miguel Leon-Portilla (1975) explains that "they expended all their efforts and energy to provide the gods with *chalchihuatl,* the precious liquid drawn from the scarified victims, the only suitable nourishment for the Sun" (37). The collaboration with and intention to preserve the life of the Sun constituted a major point in the Aztec conception of the world. Human sacrifice arose out of a basic premise, a recognition of the active role and responsibility of people for the maintenance of cosmic balance. Leon-Portilla quotes from Alfonso Caso y Andrade's great *La religión de los aztecas* (1936):

> The youthful warrior [...] is born every morning from the womb of the old earth goddess and dies every night in order to illumine the world of the dead with his faded light. But upon being born the god has to fight with his brothers, the stars, and with his sister, the moon; and, armed with the fire serpent—the solar rays—every day he puts them to flight, and his victory signifies

a new day of life for men. [...] Every day this divine battle takes place; but in order for the sun to triumph it is imperative that he be strong and vigorous, for he must fight against the countless stars... Therefore man must give food to the sun, which, being a god, disdains the coarse food of man, and can be sustained only by life itself, by the magic substance which is found in man's blood, the *chalchíuatl*, the "precious liquid," the terrible nectar which nourishes the gods. The Aztecs, people of Huitzilopochtli, are the chosen people of the sun, entrusted with nourishing him (Leon-Portilla, 215 f.).

Once Bernabe's heart is torn out in the climax of the ritual, he is resurrected as "a complete man" (*Bernabe*, in *Early Works*, 165) and the earth becomes virgin again. As her father admits: "La Tierra es virgen y tuya" (*ibid.*). La Tierra gives herself to the new Bernabe, complying with the Sun's orders that they "tengan hijos... muchos hijos"—which can be translated as "have children... lots of children" (*ibid.*). The message is clear: "The Chicano must give himself up to his indigenous roots, have faith and pride in his history, in order to again claim the land and create a new civilization of people" (*El Movimiento Chicano*, website), inhabited by people like the new Bernabe, who claims: "If once I was a loco, I am a man—and I belong to La Tierra, as she belongs to me" (*Bernabe*, in *Early Works*, 166). When Bernabe promises to love his bride "*hasta la muerte*" ("till death"), her face is turned into "a death mask" (*ibid.*). By the end of the ritual, the two embrace as a symbolic union between Man and Earth, Bernabe thus merging with the universe. The end of the play witnesses Bernabe's sacrifice and resurrection and the resultant purification of La Tierra.

Scene seven takes us back to *barrio* life, and we see the realistic version of what people think happened to Bernabe. Bernabe's relatives found him "buried in the earth" (167). They think that he was suffocated in the hole, but according to

Valdez's neo-Mayan philosophy: "Bernabe is only dead on the material level, not on the spiritual plane" (Huerta 2000, 40). His death unifies man, the earth, and the whole universe to bring about complete harmony of all things. This corresponds with Valdez's belief in the Chicano as a "universal / cosmic entity" (Morton, 1974, 73).

In *The River People*, Oddoul similarly attempts to recreate a Nubian myth—inhabited by supernatural beings—by incorporating Nubian icons and concepts. He attributes his inspiration to "the Nubian mythical and supernatural heritage" (*Nubian Writers and Racist Critics,* 2006, 36). By combining contemporary situations with mythical figures, Oddoul expands his audiences' awareness of Nubian thought and culture. As Nadia El-Banhaway (1993), in her Afterword to the play, comments: "The play derives its literary significance from dealing with a mythic theme as an objective correlative. It relies heavily on the realistic Nubian heritage braided with mature romantic rhythm." The play, which is divided into four acts leading to the drowning of the central character, can be safely described as poetic realism or mythical realism due to the often heightened language and the romantic setting, which is a stylized representation of a typical lush, sleepy Nubian Nileside village. We can smell the Nubian mudbrick walls of the villages that once dotted the banks of the Nile, and feel the warmth of the unique Nubian spirit. Oddoul also employs as much spectacle as possible. As was the case in *Bernabe*, the Nubian costumes and scenic elements reinforce cultural images and reveal resistance to the dominant culture. In addition, Nubian ritual dances and music, perpetuated from generation to generation, like wedding ceremonies, sorrowful farewell songs, and the perch dance, lavishly embellish the scenery. Such dances are far from being folkloric exhibitions, they harmonize man with nature by moving certain natural forces. Sounds of tambourines, men's clapping and stamping the ground and women's ululations help set the mood and give the play a unique flavor. The writer's use of the Nubian music and dance, reminders of their indigenous heritage, tells of Nubian identity.

In spite of the play's realistic mode of representation, it is grounded in Oddoul's belief in the mythical dimension of the Nile and the River People. As he maintains:

> I still believe in stories about the Nile's creatures. My own parents believed that there were evil beings called Amoun Dugur living there. Such stories were inherent in their daily lives. My parents used to throw pieces of bread into the Nile to appease these evil beings. They never ate any fish, nor did they throw any waste into the Nile (quoted in Amin 2002, website).

It is not only the Nile that is telling us about the inseparable and intimate interchange between the Nubians and their environment; we can also find the palm-trees, which represent another major element in any Nubian context. The very first page of the play sets the scene for the centrality of these environmental elements in the lives of the Nubians. In the description of the setting, references are made to the palm-tree lovers that represent the two lovers in the play: Asha Ashry and Siyam. As Oddoul comments in his book *Nubian Writers and Racist Critics* (2006): "The two palm-tree lovers stand for Asha and Siyam and how Siyam's long journey leads to Asha's tragic downfall, as she is leaning on him" (71).

The characters in *The River People* are Muslims, yet they still have unshakeable faith in the existence of the underwater world, which they regard as an extension of their own, with all its inhabitants like mermaids, genies of the water, and the River People. The power of unseen River People permeates the world of the central character, Asha Ashry, as well as that of her late aunt, after whom she was named. Exactly like her aunt, Asha is "deeply in love with the river and the River People." Also similar to her aunt, she adores "the perch and their dance, fights with the fishermen and throws their fish back to the Nile." The river and its people were the aunt's true love reincarnated until she "drowned herself in the Dam's year" (*The River People*, 22), after being locked up in her house and prevented from sitting on the bank of the river. Like the perch, she was suffocated between the walls and sneaked out one night and drowned herself in the Nile to live forever in bliss among the River People, whose life knows no end of joy and whose tambourines are never silent; they are unworried about the fear of a bleak future that threatens them with rupture from their roots.

From the very beginning of the play, Asha appears to be "walking in her aunt's footsteps" (*ibid.*); "doomed to her destiny" (23), as her grandmother Korty proclaims. In spite of Korty's desperate attempts to keep Asha away from the river and its people, she fails because as she desperately admits: "Their love runs in her blood exactly like my sister, Asha" (*ibid.*). In fact, Asha's destiny has been sealed long before her birth. Both Asha and her aunt symbolize the decay of the traditional Nubian life-style in the face of the encroachment of the Aswan Dam and the High Dam. For them, as for all Nubians, the dams are far from being concrete buildings that regulate the Nile's water; they are "mythical creatures...two bloody deformed ogres which inflict poverty and uprootedness upon the Nubians and devour their future" (Oddoul, *Nubian Writers,* 95).

Asha can be regarded as an "archetypal" Nubian, seeking connection with Nature's force—the Nile and the palm-trees—that speak directly to her. She is equated with Mother Nature. If Bernabe is wedded to the land, Asha is wedded to the Nile and all its creatures. According to Ibrahim Sharawey (1984) the Nubians believe not only in the existence of the underwater world but also in spirit incarnation—a remnant of a totem religion. The spirits of those underwater people will be reincarnated in the fish. Regarding the fish as underwater people reincarnated, the Nubians vehemently refuse to eat them, fearing that they might be eating the River People's flesh, with whom they are strongly bonded (91, 132).

Like Bernabe, Asha is mobile and constantly passes from one world to the other. She declares her affinity with the fish because, as she says: "I can hear the fish's cry for help and understand their screams" (*The River People,* 18). She is tormented as she sees them "shiver, suffer, and suffocate" (17), when the fisherman, Gergeda, catches them. She even likens herself to a "fish" and asks Siyam: "Will you let a fisherman catch me and separate us?" (18). Simultaneously she expresses her unwavering belief in the River People's ability to punish any fisherman who thinks about disturbing them. As she says: "Gergeda is hard-hearted. How dare he kill the fish? The River People will never leave him go unpunished! Isn't it enough, what they have inflicted upon his son, Clow?" (11) She also compares herself to one of the palm-tree lovers; she sees herself as the middle one, while Siyam is the tall one. She addresses the tall palm-tree, saying: "Don't you know that this poor palm-tree is leaning over you? Don't you know that without you she'll die?" (43). Siyam represents the best and the worst of humanity in Asha's world, for he is Nature personified as Man.

Asha is the only one who sympathizes with Clow, "the Well's Child", whom—they all believe—has gone mad because "the well's guard possessed him" (14). Asha believes that he "was punished in lieu of his father" (15). Clow, who rides a stick as if it were a donkey, has supernatural powers that allow him to make predictions. Like Bernabe, Clow is another universal symbol of innocence and purity. The villagers believe that he always "says the truth" (26). For example, he gives a piece of paper to whoever is going to get married and speaks mysterious words and then time brings them to pass. He predicts that nobody will marry Asha and prophesizes her sealed fate: "Asha is destined to marry the River People" (12). Another prophecy that will come true is that "the flood will come from the west" (28), a message which all villagers except Asha receive with sarcasm because the flood always comes from the south. Although Clow is mocked as an "idiot", Asha regards him as "blessed" (31). In spite of being mentally retarded, he, like Bernabe, commands our attention by his simplicity and directedness.

Again, like Bernabe, Asha is in direct touch with her cultural roots, which heightens her spirituality. The tension causes people to stigmatize her derisively: "You'll be an idiot like Clow" (18), or, she is "possessed by the River People" (19). Her unwavering belief in the River People symbolizes a life force to which only she can be reconciled. Being in direct contact with nature triggers heartless criticism from the villagers. Saleh, in love with her, describes her as "insane" and as a "child" who "wastes her time swimming with the fish and circling around two palm-trees; whispering to them as if they could listen to her" (41). On the material plane everyone regards her as crazy, laughing at her declaration of love for the river and its people. On the spiritual plane she feels that they are inseparable: she is one of them and they are part and parcel of her very existence.

Asha's name is never uttered unless it is followed by the Nubian word "ashry", which means beautiful. "Desired by all the village men" (31), she turns down marriage proposals and waits for years for the safe return of her Siyam, from Alexandria, where he migrated after the construction of the dam. It is worth noting that since the turn of the century, when the first barrage was constructed at Aswan, the arable lands of the Nubian valley, never plentiful, have been progressively diminished by the reservoirs of ever-higher dams. This steady encroachment culminated in the High Dam, which has finally flooded the entire region of Egyptian Nubia. The unseen destroyer of people's lives, the High Dam is the reason why the young man has gone north to get a job and left his childhood love behind. Asha hates the Dam for splitting lovers, blocking the life flow of the Nile, and polluting its sweet water. For her as well as for all Nubians, peace and purity are gone forever.

In his play, Oddoul breaks the Nubian silence by letting them tell their version of the story. When the Omda has received the news of the completion of the dam, Abdel Gabar complains: "After building the dam, every flood eats up a new piece of our land" (37). Siyam repeats the same idea: "Half of our land has drowned" (44). The tragic result is not only losing the land but also the village's men, who migrate to the north to work as servants and doormen. The dam splits up lovers. Yet Asha feels that this is an evil omen because if he leaves she'll never marry him.

Asha complains that Siyam has not listened to Korty's advice when she warns him:

> Siyam, my son, beware Alexandria's salty water. Never drink it, as it won't quench your thirst and it will eat away your intestines... Its air is so soggy that if you fill your chest with it, your southern blood will clot and your feet will stiffen on its stand and you'll never return back to us (56).

Korty's advice still carries the traces of the Ancient Egyptian's terrible dread of the Mediterranean Sea, or what they called "the Great Green" or "the greedy monster" threatening to cover the whole precious "Black Land" (Pinch 2004, 59).

Asha knows, from rumors, that Siyam has found other women in the city on the sea, but while her friends give up on their absent men and marry available locals, she remains true to her dream. When the play, itself a modern myth, tells us what happens, it does not always tell us why the people in the story do what they do or how they feel about what happens to them. As the action unfolds, and after the passage of so many years, Asha, grey-haired and very close to the menopause, is still waiting for Siyam. Nothing has changed in her. As her friend, Nafisah, says: "You're still sitting by the river's bank, whispering to the perch" (*The River People*, 87). Finally, Clow approaches her with a wet paper, which in itself is a sinister omen of what will happen to both Siyam and Asha. She shares the incredible news with those she loves most: "You River People, mermaids, my beloved perch, Siyam is coming" (94). But the news that Siyam will finally return in the next mail boat is soon followed by the sorrowful news of his drowning after the boat has sunk. Siyam's tragic life and death foreshadow the tragedy of many Nubians' demise.

The final scene of the play, the climactic moment, represents a fusion of self with place. Asha, defeated in the real world but not in the one of her beliefs, flees first to the palm-tree lovers and embraces the male tree, as if she were squeezing Siyam between her arms, till the tree's scales dig into her flesh. Then she runs off to the Nile to be with Siyam and the River People. Like the Tierra for Bernabe, the Nile becomes her mythic womb. If she is denied the fulfillment of her dream in the real world, she creates it in her own way. She opens her grandmother's jewelry chest and fastens the "disk of the Almighty" on the middle of her forehead. Covered with gold, she appears as a perfect bride waiting for her groom. She, enacting in her mind a traditional Nubian marriage ritual, consoles herself that if the villagers are not attending her wedding, she will be in the safe company of the River People and the perch that will sing and dance for her and Siyam. Rejecting the idea that Siyam, the clever river swimmer, has drowned, Asha believes that he is with the River People, waiting for her. She addresses him: "I'm your wife, Siyam. This is the disk of the Almighty, worn only by the married women. And I'm your wife today after long deprivation. I'm a perfect bride, the South's bride." And she begs him:

> Take the sword from me; raise it up to your guests as a symbol of power and protection. Sing Siyam and raise your sword, O groom. Tonight I'll carry your child in my womb... and give birth to him... chew one of our sweet dates and wet his mouth with it because I want dates to be the first thing he tastes. This will make him never forget his future sweetheart. I'll put him naked on the bank of the river because I want the golden mud of our Nile to be mixed with his marrow bone. In this way, he'll never forget his home (108 f.).

Asha moves down to the River, "singing and moving the sword until she disappears" (109). The image of Asha's drowning herself in the Nile amid the lamps and flaming torches, the men's flowing white gallabaiyas, the hoarse cries in the throats of men, sharp ones in the women's and Anna Korty's heart-rending cries and tearful pleas is a powerful literary moment. By drowning herself in the Nile, she becomes one of the River people because, as she believes: "If I drowned in the flood, I would become a fish, a perch that swims in our Nile. I would live with the River People and never leave my home" (46).

Asha, like Bernabe, merges with the universe, the individual fuses with the cosmos. Both are dead in the "reality" of thought, but in their vision they live on. All I need point out here is that the same forms appear in many different places, in response to human experiences that appear to be similar on at least one level, and that they take on different meanings to the extent that those experiences turn out to be dissimilar on other levels.

After analyzing the dynamics of myth in *Bernabe* and *The River People*, it becomes clear that there is an "archetypal" pattern that unites them, as each, in its own way, explores the relationship between Man and Earth, the known and the unknown, and each also searches for identity in the broad context of the struggle between order and chaos. That the myths presented are Chicano and Nubian does not negate the fact that the story they convey belongs to us all. It is what Joseph Campbell (1949) describes as "the wonderful song of the soul's high adventure" (19).

The myths represented in the two plays bring together in a single potent vision elements of historical fact and legendary elaboration to create an overriding commitment and bond for the community and pay homage to the Chicano and Nubian heritages. The social world represented in the writings of Valdez and Oddoul is an emphatically political one. Yet, the very act of representation encourages in us a distinctive kind of political consciousness through the deliberately constructed set of mythic productions.

References

Amin, Nour. "I Have a Dream." In: *Egypt Today: The Magazine of Egypt,* September 2002. Website, <http://www.mafhoum.com/press3/111C34.htm>

Anderson, Benedict. *Imagined Communities: Reflections on the Origin and Spread of Nationalism.* London: Verso, 1983.

Anzaldua, Gloria. *Borderlands / La Frontera.* San Francisco: Aunt Lute Books, 1987.

Brennan, Timothy. "The National Longing for Form." In: *Nation and Narration.* Ed. Homi K. Bhabha. London: Routledge, 1991, 44-70.

Broyles-Gonzalez, Yolanda. "What Price Mainstream?: Luis Valdez' *Corridos on Stage and Film.*" In: *The Chicana/o Cultural Studies Reader.* Ed. Angie Chabram-Dernersesian. New York: Routledge, 2006, 269-82.

Campbell, Joseph. *The Hero with a Thousand Faces* (1949). Princeton, NJ: Princeton University Press, 1968.

De Vidas, Anath Ariel. "The Culture of Marginality: The Teenek Portrayal of Social Difference." In: *Ethnology,* 41, 3, 2002, 209.

Doniger, Wendy. *The Implied Spider: Politics and Theology in Myth.* New York: Columbia University Press, 1998.

Huerta, Jorge. *Chicano Theater: Themes and Forms.* Ypsilanti, MI: Bilingual Press, 1982.

------------. "The Influences of Latin American Theater on *Teatro Chicano.*" In: *Mexican American Theatre: Then and Now.* Ed. Nicolas Kanellos. Houston, TX: Arte Publico Press, 1983, 68-77.

------------. *Chicano Drama: Performance, Society and Myth.* Cambridge: Cambridge University Press, 2000.

Hurwitt, Robert. "Introduction." In: *West Coast Plays, 19/20.* Ed. Robert Hurwitt. Berkeley, CA: California Theatre Council, 1986,.

Hutchinson, John. *Modern Nationalism.* London: Fontana, 1994.

Lavie, Sandra / Swedenburg, Ted. "Introduction". In: *Displacement, Diaspora, and Geographies of Identity.* Ed. Sandra Lavie / Ted Swedenburg. Durham, NC: Duke University Press, 1996, 1-25.

Leeming, David Adams. *The World of Myth.* New York: Oxford University Press, 1992.

Leon-Portilla, Miguel. *Aztec Thought and Culture: A Study of the Ancient Nahuatl Mind.* Transl. Jack Emory Davis. Norman, OK: University of Oklahoma Press, 1975.

Lévi-Strauss, Claude. "The Structural Study of Myth" (1955). In: Claude Lévi-Strauss. *Structural Anthropology.* Volume one. Transl. Clair Jacobson and Brooke Grundfest Shoepf. New York: Basic Books, 1963, 206-31.

McRobbie, Angela. "Strategies of Vigilence: An Interview with Gayatri Chakravorty Spivak." In: *Block*, 10, 1985, 5-9.

Miles, Helen. "A Lost Ancient Land." In: *The Middle East*, 236, July-August 1994, 35-7.

Morton, Carlos. "The Teatro Campesino." In: *The Drama Review*, 18, 4, December 1974, 71-6.

Movimiento Chicano, El: The Art of Revolution. Website, <http://xroads.virginia.edu/~UG01/voss/paper.html>

Oddoul, Haggag Hassan. *The River People.* With an Afterword by Nadia El-Banhaway. Cairo: The General Egyptian Organization for Books, 1993. [Arabic text]

------------. "Nubian Literature; Approaching the Headwaters." In: *Al Gasra*, 14, Fall 2002, 17-24. [Arabic text]

------------. *The Role of the Nubian Writer.* Website, 2006 [Arabic text], <http://www.nubian-forum.com/vb/showthread.php?t=75&page=2>

------------. *About Nubia and Bahaa Taher.* Website, 2006 [Arabic text], <No longer online>

------------. *Nubian Writers and Racist Critics.* Cairo Garden City: The Cairo Center for Human Rights Studies, 2006. [Arabic text]

Orona-Cordova, Roberto. "Zoot Suit and The Pachuco Phenomena: An Interview with Luis Valdez." In: *Mexican*

American Theatre: Then and Now. Ed. Nicolas Kanellos. Houston, TX: Arte Publico Press, 1983, 95-111.

Pinch, Geraldine. *Egyptian Myth: A Very Short Introduction.* Oxford: Oxford University Press, 2004.

Ramirez, Elizabeth. "Chicano Theatre Reaches the Professional Stage: Luis Valdez's *Zoot Suit.*" In: *Teaching American Ethnic Literatures: Nineteen Essays.* Ed. John R. Maitino / David R. Peck. Albuquerque, NM: University of New Mexico Press, 1996, 193-207.

Shang, Theodore J. "A Return to Aztec and Mayan Roots." In: *The Drama Review,* 18, 4, December 1974, 56-70.

Sharawey, Ibrahim. *Superstition and Mythology in Nubia.* Cairo: The General Egyptian Organization for Books, 1984. [Arabic text]

Valdez, Luis. *Early Works: Actos, Bernabe* and *Pensamiento Serpentino.* Houston, TX: Arte Publico Press, 1990.

------------. *Bernabe.* In: *West Coast Plays, 19/20.* Ed. Robert Hurwitt. Berkeley, CA: California Theatre Council, 1986, 21-51.

Walker, Steven F. *Jung and the Jungians on Myth: An Introduction.* London: Routledge. 2002.

Wiley, Catherine. "Teatro Chicano and the Seduction of Nostalgia." In: *Melus,* 23, 1, 1998, 99-115.

This essay was originally published in the *Bulletin of the Faculty of Arts,* Alexandria University, 3, 58, 2008, 1-39. It is republished here in slightly revised form by kind permission of the publisher, The Faculty of Arts, Alexandria University.

INTERCULTURALISM AND INSTITUTION-BUILDING

THE SCILET STORY
BY PREMILA PAUL

INDIA IS KNOWN for its diverse cultures, religions and languages. With the British invasion, the English language seeped into India's matchless multilingualism. When the British finally left, Indians refused to let go of English. They indigenized it and claimed it as their own. Less than three per cent of Indians can claim proficiency in English, but the demographic reality makes that group the second-largest English-speaking population in the world.

There are 22 official Indian languages and more than 330 others—both spoken and written. The British may have employed divisiveness for strategic reasons, but ironically it is English that has remained to serve as India's interstate link language enabling mobility and enhancing employability within and outside India. So English is not a minority language. There is an enormous amount of good literature produced in every Indian language, but it is often not accessible to people living even in the neighboring states. English makes pan-Indian readership possible.

Translation is a vital necessity and is a creative activity enabling readers to participate in new experiences and transform themselves as informed people. One is grateful to be able to read the works of Mahasweta Devi, O. V. Vijayan, U. R.

Ananthamurthy or Vijay Tendulkar and participate in a collective identity as Indians. Translators like A. K. Ramanujan, Lakshmi Holmström, Gayatri Chakravorty Spivak and Gita Krishnankutty and institutions like the Sahitya Akademi have thrown open the best in regional literatures to the rest of India and to the world. Workshops are periodically conducted by universities and other organizations to promote competent translations of the abundant outstanding literature available in regional Indian languages. Awards and fellowships are instituted to recognize and encourage translators.

English has become indispensable for both artistic and utilitarian purposes. Despite the insularity and parochialism encouraged by the politicians, English flourished in India and recreated itself as an Indian language. Indians are basically bilingual and many Indian writers felt a compulsive inner need to use English for their creative expression. But the detractors of Indian literature in English called it a mongrel branch of literature. They believed that Indians might successfully use English for their professional needs but could not emote in it. Early Indian writers were anxious to use "proper" English and thereby meet the standards of the master. They judged their own proficiency in English in terms of its closeness to British English. The standard was already set and the writer could only aspire to get closer to it. This imitative trend changed after Independence and Indians dared to be themselves in their creative expression. They realized the inadequacy of the King's (Queen's) English for effectively capturing the struggles and aspirations of the uneducated working class. In the Forties and Fifties, novelists like Raja Rao and Mulk Raj Anand consciously incorporated the speech rhythms and syntactical patterns of Indian languages into English and made the experiences of common people come alive in Indian English.

In the Eighties, the hesitant, conscious experimentation in the use of English gave place to a confident, assertive, unselfconscious and even playful use of English well-suited for creative writing. Refreshing Englishes and vibrant literatures emerged from different parts of India, energizing English itself. English proudly bore the diverse stamp of India. Glossaries were no longer appended to novels demanding creative reader participation. The publication of Salman Rushdie's *Midnight's Children* in 1980 liberated a whole new generation of writers from the western canon. The novel continues to make news, continues to inspire award committees, critics and creative writers. Another Indian novel that continues to elicit similar excitement and enthusiastic critical response is Arundhati Roy's *The God of Small Things* (1997). Writers like Amitav Ghosh and Vikram Seth have also become iconic figures in the international literary scene. The publication boom in Indian English literature continues. Indian writers are pursued by publishers with assurances of fat royalties, fabulous advances and huge sums for translation and film rights.

Readers, teachers and researchers of Indian literature were aware of the publication wave and the well-deserved recognition it received but found it difficult to buy or find all the books so as to undertake systematic study of them. The American Studies Research Center (ASRC), later renamed the Inter-University Center for International Studies (Iucis), and the libraries of the US consulates in major cities took care of the research interests of those working on American subjects. The British Council catered to the academic needs of scholars in British literature. The Shastri Indo-Canadian Institute popularized Canadian literature by sponsoring conferences, cultural and academic exchange programmes on the subject. The embassies and consulates of most countries in India built libraries of their own. Professor C. D. Narasimhaiah started a resource center, Dhvanyaloka, and its journal, *The Literary Criterion*, to bring together literatures produced in the former British colonies with a similar history and also the avid readers of the same for discussion, and thus enabled networking of an academic community. Dr. G. S. Balarama Gupta did more than could be expected of an individual and promoted the reading of Indian literature through the National Institute for Research in Indian

English Literature (NIRIEL) and its *Journal of Indian Writing in English*, as early as the Seventies.

Given the diversity and prolificacy of Indian literature there was plenty of space for more work. In 1985, the Study Center for Indian Literature in English and Translation (better known by its acronym, SCILET) emerged under the leadership of Dr. Paul L. Love and Professor R. Padmanabhan Nair, with the encouragement of the American College in Madurai where SCILET is located and where these two teachers had earlier helped to establish a postgraduate English department. The United Board for Christian Higher Education in Asia in New York gave seed money to launch this project and sustained its efforts in meaningful ways in later years. A few students with their youthful energy stayed on after completing their postgraduate degrees to offer enthusiastic assistance. Progressing from the hand-typed card catalog of 200 books to maintaining an automated author-subject-title catalog of more than 12,000 books and back issues of 75 journals has been an arduous task for SCILET, which functions with just ten committed members of staff, little technical help and limited resources. But as a team we have derived enormous fulfillment in watching the library and its activities grow every year and seeing it being avidly used throughout the year. On some busy days, there is standing-only-room for the users, who are happy just to be able to browse that day.

SCILET offers distance services as well. We send checklists on authors and photocopies of unavailable material as far as copyright law permits. At present we have regular users from 21 states of India and from 12 different countries. Researchers who come from distant states or countries confirm their visit well in advance to assure themselves of working space and library services. The Fulbright-Hayes Foundation has supported the visit of high school teachers—one group from Wisconsin and another from Chicago—to SCILET for a short term program, an Introduction to Indian Literature in English. These teachers stayed on for consultations and made extensive use of the library to identify study materials best-suited to create an awareness of other cultures in their students.

Scholars from Sri Lanka, Australia, New Zealand, Germany, France, Finland, the UK, the United States and Canada have all spent extended time in SCILET to write books or collect material for them. They have all acknowledged with gratitude the luxury of finding all that they wanted in a small, warm, friendly library in Madurai, a city known for its ancient culture and hospitality. Web dependent researchers from other countries find it refreshing to be able to pick up the books and journals they had been looking for from the nearby shelves. They settle down for a long reading session in their reserved carrels and grow quite possessive of them! They return every year for a month or more to work on their research papers or books. On request, SCILET helps in establishing contact or arranging interviews with contemporary Indian authors for these scholars. Some of these overseas scholars have become good friends of SCILET and have become very involved in its activities. Apart from helping us to widen SCILET's network worldwide, they have also helped us with ways of locating and procuring rare books and materials.

Several leading Indian writers have chosen to launch their books before an enthusiastic SCILET audience, and many more have offered to do so. So we hope to arrange more book launches in future. Recognizing SCILET's commitment, some of the major Indian writers have sent the original drafts of their works, often handwritten, their correspondence with other writers, letters, private diaries, photographs, *etc.* for safe keeping. We now have an enviable collection of archive material. We are honored by the trust that these highly acclaimed writers have placed in us and we want to preserve these manuscripts for posterity in the best possible manner.

Every year SCILET invites to the American College one or more creative writers to read from their works and interact with an audience that will include students, teachers and researchers from different places who are interested in that particular author's works. These "Meet the Author" sessions are highly appreciated by both academic scholars and the local public. The well-attended SCILET programs and the network of library users from near and far have helped build a community of Indian literature lovers. On December 2nd, 2010, when SCILET inaugurated the celebration of its Silver Jubilee with a lecture by the renowned novelist and political historian, Nayantara Sahgal, it was attended by more than 500 people.

Once a year, a writer is invited to lead a three-day creative writing workshop for the students of the American College and Kodaikanal International School, an institution that draws cultures and students from forty countries. Follow-up writing sessions are conducted throughout the academic year for the students. Every year a collection of the creative work that they produce is published as *Kavithalaya*. SCILET has also conducted excellent seminars sponsored by leading publishers, Sahitya Akademi and the Fulbright Foundation on such topics as *Translation, Children's Literature in India, "The West" in the Indian Imagination 1857-1947* and *Representations of the Family in Indian Literature in English*. Eminent scholars from different parts of India have participated and offered presentations in these seminars.

Sensing the need for a journal to publish significant Indian poetry and responsible criticism of the same, SCILET in 1988 launched *Kavya Bharati*, with the editorial assistance of the well-known Indian poet Jayanta Mahapatra. From 1991 up to the present, Professor R. Padmanabhan Nair has sustained its publication with his able editorship. He widened the scope of the journal to include not only poetry from different parts of India but also the poetry of the Indian Diaspora. *Kavya Bharati* has readers and subscribers in every state and union territory of India and in twenty countries overseas. Its special issues on *Translation* and *Poetry of Indian Women* and the two volumes of *Poetry of the Indian Diaspora* refuse to become back numbers, such is the volume of requests for these issues.

In its rich holdings, SCILET's library has books on Indian History, Indian Religions, Indian Philosophy, and Indian Cinema. It has also developed a significant satellite collection on Indian Women and Gender Studies. This is a much sought after and much visited section by researchers. This led to the United Board for Christian Higher Education in Asia (that originally helped establish SCILET) encouraging us to conduct a workshop on *Gender and Development in Asian Literature* in 2007. Teachers representing nine Asian countries made presentations during the event. The three-day program created in us a new awareness of SCILET's identity and the need for its existence in the broader Asian context. The discussions stimulated us to create small sections with the literatures produced in different Asian countries. We have a significant collection of literature from Pakistan, Bangladesh and Sri Lanka. We have progressed sufficiently to open a modest section of Chinese and Japanese literature as well. We plan to start our collection of Filipino literature this year.

SCILET realizes that the reward for good work is more work. We are bursting with books in just one wing of the first floor in the New Building of the American College, Madurai. Space and money are both hard to come by. Our holdings of journal back issues are being digitized to save space. But we certainly do not want to lose SCILET to cyberspace. We want to maintain the empirical interactive space of SCILET for scholars and writers. With further technical assistance, some of our services will eventually go on line but SCILET will remain a welcoming resource center affirming intercultural relationships.

THE WONDROUS
WAYS OF LOVE

BY JÜRGEN EINHOFF

WHAT'S THE POINT of another essay on love? "Isn't love the same everywhere? What is he on about?" the editor of *Praxis*, a German language teaching journal, is supposed to have asked his co-editor after I had submitted my essay "Multikulturelle Kompetenz—in der Liebe" ("Multicultural Competence—in Love") for publication. The editor did not publish it, but it was later accepted by the editors of a different language teaching journal (Einhoff 1995).

What made me take an interest in the complex topic of love was the fact that I had married a young lady from London, who had quite spontaneously and naively come to Germany without knowing what she was letting herself in for. She did not speak any German and had only rudimentary knowledge of Germany's society, its culture, history and politics. Needless to say she was not always that happy in the *Vaterland*, but she survived all the stresses and pains by—as one English visitor observed—creating a little corner of England in Germany, with five children to fill it.

"Manners maketh man" is the motto of Winchester College, and to be a gentleman is the English educational ideal for men. My background was a different one, and so I could not quite live up to the expectations of an English lady. The conflicts caused by the cultural differences were painful at times and made me look for explanations and solutions. Biology, psychology and sociology seem to offer the most convincing ones. Humberto Maturana's and Francisco Varela's concept of autopoiesis, their theory of cognition, Gregory Bateson's application of cybernetics to the field of ecological anthropology in his *Steps to an Ecology of Mind* (1972), Mara Selvini Palazzoli's family therapy, based on Bateson's systemic approach, and Niklas Luhmann's sociological systems theory all made me aware that societies and social systems in general, families included, are autopoietically (self-referentially) closed systems with unique identities and separated from one another. Each system works according to its own codes. Within a social system all social subsystems are interconnected and function according to the codes that determine the whole system. For example, the most important code of the American social system is money, which originates in the Puritan belief that possession of material goods, of money, is a sign of God's blessing. Almost as important are the codes derived from the frontier experience, *e.g.*, rugged individualism, self-reliance, can-do-spirit, physical prowess, and so on.

This is, of course, a very simplified version of systems theory and its application, but it helped me to understand the causes of our family conflicts. We had become victims of what Huntington would have called "a clash of civilizations". This can also occur, of course, within German society, between (for instance) people from the south of Germany and those from the north, but in a milder form.

Systems theory and its assumptions made me delve deeper into the causes of our experiences. Above all, I wanted to find out how the codes of a cultural system influence the relationship between the sexes, in particular love relationships. Niklas Luhmann's publication *Liebe als Passion* (1982, "Love as Passion") was very helpful in this context. For Luhmann, concepts of love are very much influenced by the society and culture in which they are found. Love as a socio-cultural phenomenon is embedded in a specific culture. It is not a feeling, but a semantic code, which generates feelings if the right code is used. The semantic codes, which—according to Luhmann—have an influence on the feelings and actions of people in love relationships, are to be found in cultural conventions (*kulturelle Überlieferungen*), in literature, in meaningful language patterns (*überzeugungskräftige Sprachmuster*) and in images of certain situations (*Situationsbilder*) (47). Concepts of love, we can assume, are related to time and space, that is to say that they differ from culture to culture, and within a culture age, gender, class and race may lead to further differentiation, and they are all subject to evolutionary change.

To do the editor of *Praxis* justice, he was not completely wrong when he reacted to my essay with the question: "Isn't love the same everywhere?", but he was not completely right, either. From a scientific point of view his question seems to be justified. Scientists assume that there are certain patterns of behavior in love relationships that people from almost all societies and cultures share and which are genetically determined and have emerged in the course of human evolution. According to socio-biologists, natural selection in general preserves those patterns of behavior that contribute the most to the survival and successful reproduction of the human race. The phenomenon of love ultimately serves this function.

It goes without saying that an essay on the complexity of the phenomenon of love cannot disregard the findings of the natural sciences, but the cultural aspect is undoubtedly of greater interest, because this is what makes love the complex phenomenon that it is.

The findings of the natural sciences will be dealt with in the next section. This will be followed by an analysis of English, Irish, and American concepts of love in connection with their respective cultural backgrounds. The focus will be on their cultural roots, and this will be illustrated by an analysis of short stories that serve as vehicles for these culturally generated concepts. This essay is not intended to give a comprehensive survey of the topic but to draw attention to the complexity of the phenomenon, showing it perhaps in a different light and encouraging the reader to think and read more about it.

Love and the Sciences

SCIENTISTS EXPLORING THE phenomenon of love have not always been greeted with enthusiasm. Two psychologists who were studying romance in the early Eighties applied for a grant and were told by Senator William Proxmire: "Right on top of the things we don't want to know is why a man falls in love with a woman" (Adler / Carey). For one thing there was confusion about whether love was an emotion or something different. Then there was the fear that the application of natural sciences like evolutionary theory to human phenomena like love might conjure up the evil spirits of Social Darwinism.

In the meantime, a lot of research has gone into the matter of love. A close connection between love and sex has been established. There is agreement among scientists that love/sex is instinct-driven and that it is potentially—through the procreation of offspring—aimed at the survival and reproduction of the human race.

In the late Eighties the psychologist David Buss tried to find out more about the genetically based behavior patterns that guided males and females in their relationships with each other. He was looking for qualities in men and women that made them sexually attractive to each other, and for those genetically transmitted traits that contributed the most to successful reproduction. These were his assumptions, seen from a Darwinian perspective:

> For a female the important thing would be to avoid squandering her limited supply of eggs. Her genetic survival would depend on finding a mate with the resources to provide for the offspring he fathers. The male's key task would be to find a female capable of bearing one. His most valuable clues about a mate

would be the physical ones suggesting fertility (Cowley).

Buss let people in 33 different societies describe their ideal mate in five categories: earning capacity, industriousness, youth, physical attractiveness and chastity. The results supported his assumptions.

> Buss found that females placed greater value on wealth and ambition while males were more sensitive to signs of youth and fertility. There was also a clean sweep on age preferences, with males preferring younger mates and females preferring older ones (Cowley).

Of course, his findings did not go undisputed at the time. But recent research has confirmed them. There is also evidence that women play a decisive role in the mating game. It is women, their choices and their sexual preferences, that push evolution along. Women act with caution and discrimination when it comes to choosing a mate and in general show a preference for male traits related to status and resource holdings (Thornhill / Gangestad, 6 ff.).

Research has also shown that women possess two sexualities. When fertile, they are most attracted by testosterone-facilitated features in a man that are markers of good genes, *e.g.*, wide shoulders and narrow waist, thicker necks, broader jaws and chins as signs of good physical strength and good health. When non-fertile, their sexuality serves the function of pair bonding and they are attracted by men who provide paternity and non-genetic material benefits and services (325 f.). Men's behavior is similar. They are attracted by oestrogen-facilitated indicators of good genes in women, *e.g.*, good looks as signals of good health and narrow waists and wide hips as indicators of fertility. It is for these reasons that they prefer young adult sex partners..

The thesis that our genetic inheritance might influence our behavior has been the subject of a recent publication in Germany and was discussed on radio and television. The birth rate in Germany has dropped dramatically in recent years. In particular, professional women seem to be affected and very often remain single and have no children. This has very often been attributed to the fact that they cannot find adequate partners to have children with. The psychologist Stefan Woinoff in his book *Überlisten Sie ihr Beuteschema* ("Outwit your Predatory Behavior Pattern") offers an explanation. He thinks it has to do with genetically transmitted behavior patterns in women and men. To his mind both sexes act according to "archaic predatory patterns", which, of course, they are quite unaware of. Women choose men who are taller and bigger than themselves, which made perfect sense in prehistoric times, when men were hunters providing for and protecting a family. They also seem to go in for men who are in a superior position, have a higher status and a high income. This also makes sense in that men of a high status will likely have good genes, which they will hand down to any offspring, and their money will assure not only the latter's survival but a better start in life. Woinoff calls this an "archaic predatory behaviour pattern", which prevents professional women from finding adequate partners, particularly since men seem to follow the completely opposite pattern. They prefer women who are inferior and who promise to be perfect bearers of their children. These women must be young, healthy and fertile (10). Of course, from an evolutionary point of view the different behavior patterns make sense and complement each other. Yet today they seem to be outdated, although they are just one of the reasons why women in higher positions have difficulties finding adequate partners to start a family with. Woinoff helps women who seek his advice to analyze their behavior patterns and modify them and find partners who live up to their *true* needs and expectations.

Woinoff's assumptions have been corroborated by research on six continents and they seem to be confirmed by the findings of the scientists quoted above.

A different aspect, "love as a chemical reaction", has been

the focus of other scientists, who normally identify three stages:

The first stage is driven by the sex hormones testosterone and oestrogen. Lust is prominent. We are love-struck, we have fallen in love. The next stage, which represents the transition from lust to love, is controlled by different chemicals called monoamines (dopamine, norepinephrine and serotin), which make us feel happy and excited. The third stage, when love becomes attachment, is controlled by the hormones oxyticin and vasopressin, which contribute to strengthening the bond between a couple (McLoughlin).

There is no denying the fact that our genetic heritage and chemical processes play an important role in the mating game, but when challenged scientists "readily concede that cultural conditions shape people's preferences. Culture, they say, is precisely the phenomenon that needs to be explained" (Cowley). This is what we shall now turn our attention to.

Love and Culture

ENGLAND: *The Historical-cultural Roots of the English Concepts of Love*

Systems theory teaches us that the culture of a nation is the result of events that shaped it in the course of history, some of which are more important than others and have a lasting effect. English society and culture were formed by a rich succession of events and forces, and yet a certain homogeneity is still apparent, due to the limited number of really significant trends and the country's island position, which allowed England for centuries to develop at its own pace with comparatively little interference from outside. (I refer to "England" and "English", since this country has always dominated the British Isles demographically, economically, militarily and culturally, but in modern times—the times of the "United Kingdom"—much of what I am discussing here can be applied to the Scots and Welsh, too.)

The events or phenomena that had the most decisive impact

on English society and culture (and therefore also on the relationships between men and women) were the Norman Conquest (1066), Christianity in its different manifestations, the Age of Reason, Romanticism, Victorianism and Industrialism.

Now that Wales and Scotland have been granted limited sovereignty and millions of immigrants from different former Commonwealth countries have become part of British life, it might be felt that English cultural hegemony and homogeneity have effectively evaporated, and with them many traditional ideas about "men and women"—but the past still lingers on!

A very important political event that left an indelible mark on English society and culture was the Norman Invasion of 1066, a major historical turning point. The Normans established a class society that has lasted almost up to the present day. It is based less on economic differences than on differences of culture. The Normans replaced the English aristocracy with a Norman-French one. The peasantry remained Saxon. The aristocracy as a ruling class continued to play a decisive role in English history and politics right up till modern times, influencing the concept of the male-female relationship. What made it different from its continental counterparts was the law of primogeniture, which meant that only the first-born son inherited the title and estates, while the other siblings were absorbed into the middle classes, with the effect of greater social intermixture. Thus the lifestyle, values, and concepts of love of the landed gentry became a model for the middle classes, too. With industrialism and the advances in the sciences and humanities at the end of the nineteenth century and the beginning of the twentieth, the traditional values of the upper and middle classes were challenged. The sexual revolution, influenced by Freud's discoveries and spurred on by the growing economic and political power of the emerging working classes, catapulted sex into the foreground of the discourse about gender relationships. But it was decades before attitudes and behavior changed.

Christianity in its different forms has probably been the most important force in the development of the traditional English attitude to love. In the Middle Ages, its concept of the soul/ body dichotomy and its emphasis on man's spirituality resulted in the emergence of the idea of non-sexual love. "Hostility to pleasure—above all, to sexual pleasure—was not merely one tenet among many of this new religion; it was central and basic" (Branden 1980, 18). In the eyes of the church, women were subordinate to men and had to obey them just as men obeyed God. Other images of women emerged. They were either seen as whores or as symbols of purity modeled on the Virgin Mary. Puritanism in the sixteenth and seventeenth centuries exacerbated the restrictive tendencies. Its intention was to purify the Church of England and, consequently, it was extremely hostile to earthly pleasures and indulgences and repressive in its regulation of sex. Marriages were not based on love but were arranged for economic and political reasons. The Age of Reason with its contempt for emotions and passions downgraded the status of women even further. Love was regarded as a game. "Women were to be flattered, fooled, manipulated, toyed with, seduced, but never taken seriously" (28). Romanticism was the obvious counter-movement to this development. Its protagonists celebrated the naturalness of passion. They stressed the free choice of lovers. The sexual act was based on mutual love and not on the consent of society.

> Their vision of love was that of a desire for union between two highly individualistic souls who had a fundamental spiritual likeness, so that finding one's "soul mate", choosing the appropriate person, was of the highest importance (33).

Shakespeare, who in his plays had already advocated love as an important precondition to marriage, was celebrated.

Victorianism can be seen as a reaction to the Romantic Movement. It tamed romantic love. Victorian love combined mutual respect, devotion and affection with marriage, but greatly inhibited sex (37 ff.). Social change and the Freudian sexual revolution eventually did away with these ideas and paved the way for more liberal attitudes towards sex and for the concept of romantic love to be the one English people go in for today.

A love relationship is normally a private matter between a man and a woman. For a woman to love a man he has to live up to certain expectations and standards and vice versa. In England a man had to be a gentleman for a woman to develop any feelings of love for him. A woman had to be a lady to be truly attractive to a man.

The gentleman ideal developed over the centuries. "The desire to be a gentleman had run through and illuminated English history from the time of Chaucer until the First World War, after which it began to die, at least as a social force" (Mason 1982, 13 f.). The word "gentleman" describes a rank in society but also a certain code of behavior. The image of a gentleman comprises both Greek elements—he should be swift, strong, brave, high-spirited, dangerous to enemies, gentle to friends, trained in body and soul, admiring beauty—and Latin ones—he should possess a sense of duty, *gravitas*, dignity, seriousness (21 f.). A gentleman embodied the concept of Courtly Love, a love not between a man and his wife but between a man and someone else's wife, a passionate spiritual love, not to be consummated. The men in Chaucer displayed chivalry, truth, honor, generous thought, courtesy, courage, skills at arms and fidelity in love (45). The men in Jane Austen's novels had to behave like gentlemen if they wanted to be accepted, which meant that they had to be sensible, to be good horsemen, be able to dance well, have a good taste in drawing and music, have principles, fidelity, staying power in love, elegance, consideration for others, kindness, tenderness, good breeding, good manners, a sense of humor, enthusiasm, warmth and style (70 ff.). The image of the gentleman did not change in its core in Victorian times. A gentleman was expected to "live consistently and intelligently, with self-respect, performing his dues; [and] show self-respect and consideration for women" and "courage"

(20). And although the gentleman ideal lost its relevance as a social force at the beginning of the twentieth century, the idea is still present in the collective subconscious of the English.

The female equivalent to the gentleman is the English lady, but unlike his image hers has undergone dramatic changes. The Renaissance, with its "cult of the woman of poise, grace, beauty, wit and erudition" (Oakley 1981, 5) elevated the status of women. In Elizabethan times, a lady had to combine

> a soft and dainty tenderness with an air of womanly sweetness. [...The] lady should avoid affectation, move gracefully, be mannerly, intelligent, neither arrogant nor envious, neither slanderous nor vain nor quarrelsome nor silly. She must be ready to talk to any man, but she must be neither indelicate nor prudish, nor catty about other women. She must have knowledge of literature, painting and music and must of course know how to dance, but above all must have virtue, so that she is honored (Mason, 55).

Puritanism in the sixteenth and seventeenth centuries downgraded the status women had enjoyed in the late Middle Ages and Renaissance. However, the Romantic Movement of the late eighteenth and early nineteenth century with its celebration of the feelings and passions of the individual upgraded their image again. Reading Jane Austen's novels as social history reminds us a little of the times of Courtly Love. Women had to be prudent, had to have a sense of propriety and elegance. They had to be principled, be good-natured, kind and motherly, show sensibility and gentility. To voice intimate feelings in their presence was regarded as vulgar (75 ff.).

Victorianism did little to dissolve the soul/body dichotomy as the dominating principle of the English concept of love. Women "were fairy-like creatures, almost unconscious of the body" (146). It was a common belief that women lacked sexual passions and consequently "girls were instructed to be modest in interactions with men and boys and sexually reserved with husbands" (Thornhill / Gangestad, 4).

Victorian women were emotionally and sexually more crippled than their counterparts in other European countries or in America. Their social status was not much better, either. Once married, Victorian women were appendixes of their spouses and had no rights. They were supposed to obey their husbands. Their role was to have children and to look after the home. Opposition to this situation began in the late 1840s, but progress was slow. When women over thirty were granted suffrage in 1918 and universal suffrage was introduced in 1928, women may have achieved political equality, but legally and socially they were still inferior. The image of the happy housewife persisted and it took until the Seventies and Eighties for Victorian attitudes to really change. The well-known phrase *No sex please, we're British!* is a reminder of a tradition that lasted for centuries. American soldiers came up against it when they were stationed in Britain during the Second World War. The young Americans were used to kissing their dates in America at a very early point in the relationship, which made English girls withdraw, because kissing—according to the scheme of British dating rituals— was the last stage but one before sex (see Watzlawick 1976, 63 f.). This gave rise to the famous English phrase criticising the Americans: *They are overpaid, oversexed, and over here.*

Today the pendulum has swung in the opposite direction. On the internet you read that English girls are not as prudish as they used to be. Most English youngsters have done away with the inhibitions that tortured their parents and can speak more openly about sexual matters. Romantic love, the "passionate spiritual-emotional-sexual attachment between a man and a woman that reflects a high regard for the value of each other's person" (Branden, 3) has become the ideal for most of them. Yet old attitudes still persist.

The Valentine Generation *(John Wain)—a Modern English Love Story*

The short story *The Valentine Generation*, first published in 1963, exemplifies in a convincing way the main-stream British concepts of love today. The story is about a postman, who for the first time in his life is faced with a dilemma situation. As he is emptying a letter-box and taking the contents to his van a young woman rushes up and begs him to give her back the letter she has just posted. He is reluctant. Regulations mean a lot to him after forty years of service, and what they tell him is that he shouldn't give in to her begging. She explains to him what happened, but he doesn't budge. However, her crying makes him stop, and they start a lively discussion about—love. Their views are completely different and it becomes obvious that they belong to different generations. The story has an open end, and we never find out whether he gives her the letter or not.

In *The Valentine Generation* John Wain is contrasting two different but both typically English concepts of love. The postman and the girl agree in that both think that the purpose of love is happiness, a stipulation of the Age of Enlightenment. (The postman: *He won't make you happy.* The girl: *But he does make me happy.*). They differ as to how happiness can be achieved. The postman pleads for the traditional concept, the Victorian concept of love. A man has to be a gentleman, caring, kind, appreciative, fair, and trustworthy, interested in a lasting relationship, in romance—and sexually inhibited. The girl on the other hand has a concept of love that emphasizes physical passion and sex. A manly and aggressive man brings out the femininity in a woman, which—in her eyes—leads to a deeper understanding on a physical level.

The two different concepts reflect not only the social dichotomy of English society, the separation into two culturally different classes, with the postman's concept being that of the upper and middle classes and the girl's concept more that of the working classes, but also the soul/body dichotomy, which has dominated the way English people speak about love, the language of love, and thus conditioned the feelings and behavior of English people in the context of love relationships.

Ireland: *The Historical-cultural Roots of the Irish Concepts of Love*

Irish society is nothing if not complex and yet if we focus on what today is the Republic and its culture we see that certain trends run through its history which have been there almost from the beginning and which —as a matter of fact—have had a determining influence on the relationship between the sexes. These are: Celtic society and culture, and Catholic Christianity.

Early Irish society was Celtic. The Gaelic Celts had come from central Europe and were survivors of Roman expansionism. They had brought with them a fully developed culture, which greatly appreciated music and poetry, traditions which have continued until today and become an element of Irishness. The Celts were also said to be great talkers and storytellers. This tradition has also continued through the ages and was—during the times of the English conquest and rule—a decisive factor in keeping the Irish language and culture alive. No wonder Irish women have always been bewitched by musicians, poets and storytellers. Pegeen, the main female character in John Millington Synge's famous play *The Playboy of the Western World* (1907), falls in love with Christy because she sees in him an excellent sportsman (as he indeed is) but also somebody who can express his love for her in the grandest poetical fashion and who impresses her with his story about hitting his father with a spade, a crime that makes him a hero among the County Mayo peasants and in Pegeeen's eyes. Christy has what the Irish call the "Gift of the Gab", or the "Blarney", the ability to eloquently and skilfully flatter or persuade a person. Pegeen's image of Christy seems to have been modeled on Cúchulainn, the arch-hero of Ireland and an ideal male figure in the eyes of many Irish women. "Cúchulainn is a kind of Old Testament Christ, mystically born, a mixture of gentleman and extreme ferocity", he never went anywhere without his hurling stick and was a champion games-player (Trevor 1984, 24). Women are said to have eyed him constantly. In Pegeen's eyes Christy is one of the "fine fiery fellows with great rages when their temper's roused". He seems to have "a mighty spirit" and "a gamey heart". She admires his "poet's talking" and "bravery of heart" and is impressed by his sporting feats: "Well, you're the lad, and you'll have great times from this out when you could win that wealth of prizes, and you sweating in the heat of noon."

The Gaels were farming people and so have the Irish been right up to recent times. Cattle were a primary source of income, and land was the basis of wealth. Land also played a decisive role when marriages were arranged. Country marriages in Ireland followed an ancient pattern. It was called match-making, and involved the respective parents, a speaker and a dowry. It was the only respectable method of marriage and the usual method of inheritance in the Irish countryside. The match begins when the farmer looks for a suitable wife for the son who is to inherit the farm. "Getting married is no carefree, personal matter; one's whole kindred help, even suggesting candidates" (O'Connor 1959, 259). The speaker conducts the negotiations between the families, inquiries are made about the candidates and a sum of money as a dowry is agreed upon. When everything has been settled, the young people are allowed to meet in the presence of family and friends. If they suit one another a day is arranged when the girl's family come to see the land. If there are no objections the wedding arrangements can then go ahead. This pattern of match-making is typical of agricultural societies, in which relationships between men and women are conceived of and defined not in terms of love but in terms of practical needs (Branden, 11).

Early Irish society was law-based and centered on the *tuath* (petty kingdom) and on the *fine* (extended family), which comprised four generations. "Most of the laws were based on the family and its relations with other families" (Coohill

2008, 10). Within the *fine*, the family unit was more important than any individual. The strong bond among its members and the strict rules on how marriages were arranged made free, romantic love almost impossible. The only way out for illicit lovers was elopement, which is a familiar motif in Irish literature and legend. Examples include the tale of Díarmuid and Gráinne (O'Farrell 1995, 29 ff.) and the story of Déirdre and Naoise (57 ff.). Díarmuid and Gráinne are regarded as the most glamorous lovers in ancient Irish legend. He was very handsome and she was the most beautiful woman in Ireland. Their elopement ended in Díarmuid's death. Déirdre was intended to marry the old king of Ulster but eloped with her young lover Naoise, who in the end was also killed.

Christianity came to Ireland in 431 AD with the mission of St. Patrick. It made a greater impact on the country than any other force, with the exception of the influence of England, which, however, did not succeed in crushing the spirit of the Irish despite centuries of occupation and oppression, so that Jill and Leon Uris could sum up the essence of Irish history in one sentence: "An unconquerable spirit endures through a tragic history" (Uris / Uris 1989, 11). The contribution of Christianity to Ireland has been commented upon by Paul F. State (2009): "The importance to Ireland's subsequent history of the coming of Christianity cannot be overstated, and the centrality of the new religion to Irish life is apparent from its very beginning on the island" (21).

Catholic Christianity survived the Viking attacks and the Norman and English invasions and plantations. The Roman Catholic faith became equated with Irishness. The influence of the church on Irish society increased with the pressure exercised by the English. The Great Famine had a particular effect in this respect.

> The combination of economic necessity and church influence led to the acceptance of a stricter moral life amongst most Irish people, and may have led to the

strong influence that the Catholic church was to have on Irish life for the rest of the first half of the twentieth century (Coohill, 91).

The influence of the church was particularly felt in the relations between the sexes, with an emphasis on purity. It contributed to Irish "momism", the doting of sexually unfulfilled mothers on their sons, urging them to become priests in order to increase their own social status (Uris / Uris, 27). It made Irish boys look on marriage as a burden, which had to be postponed. The Irish definition of a "queer" is revealing in this respect: "A man who prefers girls to drink."

Today the influence of the church has declined, and birth control and divorce have been accepted, although abortion is still illegal. Socio-economic changes and globalization have changed Ireland and have linked it "more closely with trends and perspectives characteristic of the modern world" (State, 309). This also applies to relationships between men and women. Irish people today go in for romantic love. Marriages are ideally based on love, more so than at any time in the past.

Lovers *(Liam O'Flaherty)—a Typical Irish Love Story*

Lovers is a short story that exemplifies the traditional Irish concept of love. It is about the encounter between the 77-year-old Michael Doyle and the 70-year-old Mary Kane, who in their youth had a passionate love affair, which came to nothing because Mary's parents objected to a marriage and forced her to marry Ned Kane, who is now dead. Mary tries to remind Michael of what happened in the past, but he has lost his memory and does not even recognize her, neither does he remember their passionate love, which is a very painful experience for her. It shows the tragic nature of romantic love relationships in the rural society of Ireland's past.

Lovers combines Celtic elements with those of the Christian tradition. What can be ascribed to the Celtic heritage of the country is the idea of love as passion, which breaks the rules and norms of a society. It endangers the power of the family, and its authority to determine the lives of the children. The story shows that free, passionate love is forbidden in a rural society and relegated to the darkness of night. (Mary: *I used to run up the little road after night.*). Their love affair has no happy end, because her parents object to Michael for social and material reasons. In their eyes Michael is a *drunkard that hasn't a shirt on his back;* Mary: *we had four cows then, and we were rich, and it was well known that I had thirty acres of land and the stock and two hundred gold sovereigns for my portion.* For Mary and Michael elopement is the only chance they have. (Mary: *You came with your relations and stole me out of the house with a strong hand... and glad enough I was to go too.*). This motif reminds the reader of the legendary figures of Ireland's prehistoric past, who eloped, but later met with a tragic fate. Mary's and Michael's relationship ends tragically, too.

Other aspects of the short story can also be traced back to the heroes of pre-historic times. Like Díarmuid, Michael was handsome. (Mary: *You had golden curls and your eyes glittered like the sea with the sun full on it.*), physically strong and powerfully built. (*you that were the pride of the parish / He had once been a man of great size...*). Like Cúchulainn he had a fiery temper and was involved in a great number of fights. (Mary: *it's all the fighting you did / and you gave Ned Kane such a beating with a stick that he spent three months in hospital.*). Michael's speech reveals rudimentarily a language that must have been powerful when he was young, connecting him to the poets and storytellers celebrated in Irish cultural history. (Michael: *I could beat with my bare hands any man in the parish that ever sucked at his mother's breast.*). Mary, too, seems to have been modeled on the heroines of the past. Like Gráinne she was beautiful when she was young. (*It was obvious that she had once very beautiful legs and her carriage was that of a woman who was once beautiful.*). And she personifies the values of the Christian heritage: gentleness, care and compassion. (Mary: *Won't you say a gentle word to me? / it's an unholy sight you are, all crippled and not knowing me. / I gave you warm milk to drink / God help you, poor man*). The idea of the transient nature of life embodied in the frail figure of Michael can also be ascribed to the Christian legacy. (*His withered countenance seemed to have lost all traces of human consciousness. It was apelike.*).

Like other Irish love stories, *Lovers* has a tragic end and involves pain and suffering. (Mary: *Oh! isn't this life cruel?/ I used to cry my eyes out then. / It's been a long and lonely life of misery I had... a sad, sad memory of love that was strangled in its cradle.*).

Yet *Lovers* does not refer to any of the physical aspects of love, which can be ascribed to the strong influence of the Catholic church in Ireland.

AMERICA: *The Historical-cultural Roots of the American Concepts of Love*

The United States is a complex multi-ethnic, multi-racial and multi-cultural society. Because of its diversity there is not just one concept of love but many, depending on the ethnic, racial or cultural background of the people. That said, however, there is still such a thing as a mainstream traditional American love concept, representative of the white Anglo-Saxon Protestant majority, which was shaped by forces dating back to the origins of the American nation and its history. The most important of these forces, which left their indelible mark not only on the culture of America and its value system but also on its concept of love are: Puritanism, the Age of Reason, the Romantic Period and the Frontier Experience.

Puritan culture has been anti-romantic in its repressive regulation of sexual behavior. Puritanism even governs the field of sexual morality today. Sex is still a taboo subject. People do not talk openly about it, but covertly in hints, insinuations and riddles. This repression of the sexual impulse has probably achieved the opposite of its intended effect, because it has made the Americans sex-obsessed and sexually possibly the most active people in the world (Gelfert 2003, 110). For Americans, being sexually active is good for your health. Many American parents even encourage their teenage children to be heterosexually active for fear that they might not turn out to be sexually "straight" (111 f.). Sarah Palin is a good example of this ambiguous attitude of Americans towards sex. She adamantly preaches good old conservative family values, and yet her daughter was pregnant at the age of seventeen. There does seem to be a certain amount of hypocrisy in America over sex.

As for relations between the sexes: the essence of the social order in the Puritan family lay in the superiority of a husband over his wife and all the other members of the family. A woman had to accept this status as a prerequisite of love, and she was expected to be a virgin when she married. Today the "Virgin Cool Movement" is a reminder of America's Puritan past.

The Puritan legacy is also important when it comes to choosing a male partner. For Puritans, someone who is wealthy and has money is blessed by God. For American women a rich man is a candidate of choice.

A key American value is egalitarianism, which originated in the Age of Reason. The American commitment to the ideals of equality, political freedom, and individualism, to the doctrine of individual rights and the belief in a person's right to pursue his or her happiness here on earth, all contributed to a decline in the influence of Puritan sexual morality, which combined with ideas of the Romantic Period paved the way for the American concept of romantic love, which sets the individual free to marry for passion and love.

The roughness of the conditions on the Frontier is reflected in the images of men and women. The frontiersman is a free, self-reliant individual, who loves the outdoors. He goes in for hunting and fishing. He is physically tough, somewhat coarse, and has no strong ties to women. He prefers the company of his buddies. At heart he remains a boy who cherishes his freedom and goes in for love only so long as it "does not compromise his freedom" (Fiedler 2003, 339). His flight from women is considered a flight from "petticoat tyranny" (342) and from "maturity and fatherhood" (317). Today this image lives on in the "good ole boy" of the South, who with his interest in guns, hunting, fishing and drinking exemplifies virility. He likes the company of his buddies and is a member of some male social group, normally a gun, rifle or hunting club.

The American woman's image of herself is that of "a culture bearer, the civilizer of her spouse" (339) on the untamed frontier. Like the frontiersman, she is strong and self-reliant. She is dominant in the house, but normally smart enough not to show her superiority in her relationships with men. Egalitarianism improved her status in society and made her into a staunch defender of the concept of romantic love. The power of American women has had a detrimental effect on men. The

> new expectations of women often result in a "male backlash" and a "flight from responsibility" exemplified by those in the various men's movements. [...] In short, for many men their sense of sexuality remains a confusing, but self-sustaining mix of predatory behavior and deep insecurity (Whitehead 2010, 168).

The End of Something *(Hemingway)—an American Love Story*

The short story *The End of Something* is about the breakup of a teenage love affair between Nick Adams and his girl-friend Marjorie. They are fishing off Horton's Bay, a former lumbering town that is now derelict. Nick gives Marjorie some useful pieces of advice about fishing. When they land on the beach for a picnic, Marjorie prepares everything and they eat in silence. When, after a quarrel, Nick voices his reservations about their relationship and tells Marjorie that love is not fun any more, Marjorie leaves. Nick's friend Bill turns up and questions Nick about how it went, but Nick tells him to go away.

In Germany, Hemingway's short story has been interpreted as the end of a fairly harmless girl-boy relationship.

> They have come to a point where their relationship will either change into something new or really come to an end. Nick seems to have rather a limited, conventional view of what a boy-girl relationship should be. The word "love", introduced by Marjorie, is only a very unspecific label (Gohrbandt 1985, 30).

American literary critics, however, see *The End of Something* as describing a relationship rather more substantial than that. For Philip Young (1966), it is "the end of a sort of love affair that an adolescent Nick has had with a girl named Marjorie" (33). For Sheridan Baker (1967), too, it is about the end of an affair: "Nick breaks off his affair with his waitress sweetheart and fishing companion" (29). For Harry Barba (1970), a love relationship has come to its natural end:

> Theirs is, after all, not an eternal relationship that might lead to a "marriage made in heaven". Their love is mortal and, like the mill, falls into disuse and ruin; their love does not participate in the immortality of the moon or romantic true love (78).

For Barry Stampfl (1991) a teenage romance has come to an end (34). And Horst H. Kruse (1967) offers the most detailed interpretation. He points out that Nick's love affair must have lasted for some time. For him it was not a "puppy-love affair with a 'nice' girl", but a love relationship that included sex (159 ff.).

The formative forces of American culture that had an impact on *The End of Something* are: Puritanism, the Age of Enlightenment, the Romantic Period, and the Frontier Experience. The Puritan heritage shows itself, above all, in the way that the protagonist speaks about sex. It is a taboo topic, even for Americans today. Nick finds it difficult to speak about it. His words are enigmatic. (Marjorie: *What's really the matter?* – Nick: *I don't know. – Of course you know. – No I don't. – Go and say it. - It isn't fun any more, not any of it.*) Marjorie seems to be less inhibited when she asks: *Isn't love any fun?*, but she also comes across as someone who is sparing with words. The two seem to be making use of a laconic mode of speaking, a legacy of the language of trappers, cowboys and adventurers on the frontier (Gelfert, 164).

For this reason we can assume that the words that Nick and Marjorie use in their conversation (*it* and *love*) do not just refer to a platonic relationship, but to a sexual one. In encoded form Nick tells Marjorie why he is not interested in a relationship any more: She has lost her virginity. When they talk about preparing a bait Nick tells Marjorie that *You don't want to take the ventral fin out,...., It'll be alright for bait but it's better with the ventral fin in.* For Kruse this is a reference to the loss of her virginity and with "having lost her virginity [...] she has lost her attraction for her lover" (161).

The frontier experience is also reflected in their characters. Nick to some extent embodies the typical traits of a frontiersman. He is familiar with his natural surroundings, has mastered the survival strategy of fishing, self-reliance is his ideal. He prefers to go it alone rather than being civilized by a woman. The flight from petticoat tyranny is a central theme in American fiction. Gelfert quotes Fiedler, who characterizes the typical American man as somebody who craves for a clean, sex-free homoerotic relationship between two buddies away from a mucky hetero-sexual one (Gelfert, 46). The end of *The End of Something* confronts us with this situation. Nick, the outdoorsman, has introduced Marjorie to the mysteries of angling and sex. As soon as his teaching has come to an end (*I've taught you every-thing*) and she makes him realize her superiority and takes the initiative, in order to tie him down into a lasting relationship, he backtracks and seeks refuge in his friendship with Bill.

Marjorie's reaction to being rejected correlates with the images of strong American women, who proved themselves on the frontier and are independent and self-confident (*Was there any scene? – No, there wasn't any scene.*). Marjorie's behavior has been shaped by the progressive concept of equality and by romantic ideas (*There's our old ruin....It's more like a castle*). For Nick she has become too powerful. (*You know* everything) She does not embody American men's secret—Puritan—ideal of the chaste woman, who is a virgin when she marries.

The aspect of wealth and money as necessary for winning a woman's love does not play a role in their relationship, as theirs is a teenage love and not meant to last for ever.

Résumé

A COMPARISON BETWEEN the traditional love concepts of England, Ireland and America reveals similarities and differences. Similarities could be expected, given the genetic heritage shared by all human beings and the Christian tradition as the determining force in all three of these cultures. Differences result from the different manifestations of Christianity in the respective countries and from factors that are unique to each of them.

In England Puritanism, the Age of Reason, Romanticism, and Victorianism shaped the traditional love concept of the upper and middle classes. The emerging working classes and their increasing influence on political decisions eventually resulted in the Freud-inspired sexual revolution cracking the prudish love concept of Victorian times.

In Ireland the Celtic heritage and Catholicism were determining factors. The Catholic Church was the decisive force during the period of English occupation and consolidated the power of the extended family as the traditional core unit in Irish society and the authority in matters of love.

Puritanism in England and Catholicism in Ireland led to concepts of love that emphasized the spiritual and "purity" aspects of love, suppressing sex. Puritanism in America had a similar effect on relationships between men and women. It made sex a taboo topic for ages. However, the ideals of the Age of Enlightenment, above all the ideas of freedom and individuality, and the frontier experience, with its celebration of the rugged individualist, weakened the influence of Puritan moral principles on the behavior of American men and women.

Material goods, wealth and money have figured prominently in the love concepts of all three societies. In England, the gentleman was expected to have enough wealth at his disposal to be able to support a family, although this was not the top priority in a lady's value system. The qualities of a gentleman were of greater importance. In Ireland, the ownership of land and farm animals was a prerequisite for match-making, irrespective of a woman's real feelings. Calvinistic Protestantism in America put wealth and money on a very high pedestal, because to be rich was a sign of God's blessing, and so American women have always tended to be attracted to such men.

Today, in the age of the internet and globalization, the concept of romantic love has spread not only to English-speaking countries but far beyond. However, this does not save people from a surprise when they discover that their partner from a different country does not live up to their expectations, which were shaped by the culture they grew up in. National mentalities die hard!

In retrospect, we can say that what appears to be wondrous in the ways of love is less so once one understands what it is that makes people develop feelings of love for one another. It is their genetic heritage that drives them but their cultural backgrounds that transform this, making the concepts of love different in different countries. This puzzles people, and they wonder what went wrong when they fall in love and later perhaps out of love with a person from a different country or cultural background. "It's the culture, Stupid!"

References

Adler, Jerry / Carey, John. "The Science of Love." In: *Newsweek*, February 25th, 1980, 53-54.

Baker, Sheridan. *Ernest Hemingway: An Introduction and Interpretation.* New York: Holt, Rinehart & Winston, 1967.

Barba, Harry. "The Three Levels of 'The End of Something'." In: *Philological Papers*, 17, 1970.

Bateson, Gregory. *Steps to an Ecology of Mind: Collected Essays in Anthropology, Psychiatry, Evolution, and Espistemology* (1972). Chicago: University of Chicago Press, 2000.

Branden, Nathaniel. *The Psychology of Romantic Love* (1980). New York: Bantam Books, 1983.

Coohill, Joseph. *Ireland: A Short History.* Oxford: Oneworld, 2008.

Cowley, Jeoffrey. "How the Mind Was Designed." In: *Newsweek,* March 13th, 1989, 36.

Einhoff, Jürgen. "Multikulturelle Kompetenz—in der Liebe." In: *Neusprachliche Mitteilungen aus Wissenschaft und Praxis,* 2, 1995, 86-92.

------------. "It's the Culture, Stupid! Hemingway's 'The End of Something' aus kulturdidaktischer Perspektive." In: *Praxis Fremdsprachenunterricht,* 5, 2006, 15-20.

Fiedler, Leslie A. *Love and Death in the American Novel.* Buffalo, NY: Dalkey Archive Press, 2003.

Gelfert, Hans-Dieter. *Typisch amerikanisch: Wie die Amerikaner wurden, was sie sind,* Munich: Beck, 2003.

Gohrbandt, Detlef. *Ernest Hemingway: The Short Happy Life of Francis Macomber and Other Stories—Model Interpretations.* Stuttgart: Klett, 1985.

Hemingway, Ernest. "The End of Something". In: *Repeat after Us.* Website, <http://www.repeatafterus.com/title.php?i=8752>

Kruse, Horst H. "Ernest Hemingway's 'The End of Something': Its Independence as a Short Story and its Place in the 'Education of Nick Adams'." In: *Studies in Short Fiction,* IV, 1967, 152-66.

Luhmann, Niklas. *Liebe als Passion: Zur Kodierung von Intimität* (1982). Frankfurt/M.: Suhrkamp, 1983.

Mason, Philip. *The English Gentleman: The Rise and Fall of an Ideal* (1982). London: Pimlico, 1993.

Maturana, Humberto R. / Varela, Francisco J. *Der Baum der Erkenntnis: Die biologischen Wurzeln des menschlichen Erkennens* [*El árbol del conocimiento*, 1984]. Munich: Goldmann, 1990.

McLoughlin, Claire. "Science of Love—Cupid's Chemistry." Website, <http://www.thenakedscientists.com/HTML/articles/article/clairemcloughlincolumn1.htm/>

Oakley, Ann. *Subject Women* (1981). London: Fontana, 1985.

O'Connor, Frank (Ed.). *A Book of Ireland.* Belfast: The Blackstaff Press, 1959.

O'Farrell, Padraic. *Ancient Irish Legends.* Dublin: Gill & Macmillan, 1995.

O'Flaherty, Liam. "Lovers." In: *Short Stories: The Pedlar's Revenge and Other Stories.* Dublin: Wolfhound Press, 1976, 105-14.

Palazzoli, Mara Selvini. *Magersucht.* Stuttgart: Klett-Cotta, 1986.

Stampfl, Barry. "Similes as Thematic Clues in Three Hemingway Short Stories." In: *The Hemingway Review,* 1, 1991.

State, Paul F. *A Brief History of Ireland.* New York: Checkmark, 2009.

Synge, John Millington. *The Playboy of the Western World: A Comedy in Three Acts* (1907). In: *Project Gutenberg,* August 27th, 2008. Website, <http://www.gutenberg.org/files/1240/1240-h/1240-h.htm>

Thornhill, Randy / Gangestad, Steven. *The Evolutionary Biology of Human Female Sexuality.* Oxford: Oxford University Press, 2008.

Trevor, William. *A Writer's Ireland: Landscape in Literature.* London: Thames & Hudson, 1984.

Uris, Leon / Uris, Jill. *.Ireland: A Terrible Beauty.* London: Corgi, 1989.

Wain, John. "The Valentine Generation" (1963). In: *Him and Her: The Relationship between the Sexes.* Ed. Friedhold Schmidt / T. Lothar Wullen. Munich: Hueber, 1979, 76-78.

Watzlawick, Paul (1976). *How Real Is Real?* London: Souvenir Press, 1983.

Whitehead, Stephen. *Men and Masculinities.* Cambridge: Polity, 2010.

Woinhoff, Stefan. *Überlisten Sie Ihr Beuteschema.* Munich: Goldmann, 2007.

Young, Philip. *Ernest Hemingway: Reconsideration.* University Park, PA: Pennsylvania State University Press, 1966.

CULTURAL IDENTITY

THE BABY AND THE BATHWATER

BY FRANCIS JARMAN

This is the slightly revised text of a presentation given at a conference in Egypt, the Second International Conference of the University of Minia: "The Arab-Western Dialog: Diversity or Divergence unto Harmony?", in March 2010. It is published with the kind permission of the conference organizer, Professor Amal Moustafa Kamal.

IN THIS TALK I'd like to follow up on a presentation that I gave here in Minia in 2006 at a previous conference, the Third International Conference of the Faculty of Al-Alsun. In that presentation I argued that the current wave of globalization is not a monolithic, Anglo-Saxon conspiracy, designed to erase all other cultures of the world and replace them with Anglophonia, McDonalds and Coca-Cola, but actually a more complex, inter-active process in which, at the center, the hegemonic culture is being altered while, at the periphery, new, culturally mixed forms are developing. The key word is *syncreticism*, meaning here the coming together and blending of disparate cultural elements.

In the history of the human race, Western hegemony is only an episode—in earlier times, a similar role was played, over large parts of the world, by Graeco-Roman culture, or later, in its dynamic, expansionist phase, by Islam. Perhaps in a hundred years from now—or even less—it will be China. In my talk I offered examples from the coinage of the ancient world, one of my favorite areas of research, to illustrate an interactive model in which there was a two-way process of give-and-take, of cross-fertilization and mutual learning, often leading to more sophisticated and syncretic solutions. Superficially, Rome and its institutions triumphed, but they were complemented, enriched, subverted and transformed by the cultures of the subjugated peoples.

Let me stay for a moment with the coins. One of my students recently completed an examination thesis in which she sought to explain the syncretic nature of early Christianity. It is no great secret that the early Church drew heavily on elements not only from earlier religions but also from rival cults. I pointed out to her how two Graeco-Roman cities of Asia Minor, Tarsus in Cilicia and Laodiceia in Phrygia, had placed on their coins the image of a syncretic goddess of Fortune who combined the features of various deities.

The coin from Tarsus, for instance, shows *Tyche*, or Fortuna, holding her characteristic rudder and horn of plenty, but incorporating also the rattle (sistrum) of the Egyptian goddess *Isis*, the wheel and the wings of *Nemesis*, or Fate, the helmet and spear of *Athena*, goddess of wisdom, and the corn-ears of *Demeter*, the goddess of nature and fertility. The wings may additionally refer to *Nike*, or Victory. The coins indicate that Tarsus and Laodiceia were not cities that were culturally narrow and closed-in, but very likely vibrant places of dialog and encounter.

Tarsus was famous for its linen, but also for items made of *cilicium*, a thick, rough cloth woven from the wool of long-haired Cilician goats. The "linen-workers" of Tarsus seem to have played a substantial role in the life of their city. The philosopher Dio Chrysostom mentioned that they were sometimes regarded as a "useless rabble" who were "responsible for the tumult and disorder" in their city (*Discourses* XXXIV, 21). Philostratus, writing in the first half of the third century, complained that the people of Tarsus attended more to their "fine linen" than the Athenians did to wisdom (*The Life of Apollonius of Tyana,* book

I, chapter 7). It so happens that Tarsus was the home city of Paul, the practical founder of Christianity—he describes it quite accurately as "no mean city" (*Acts of the Apostles* 21: 39)—, and Paul himself came from a family of tent-makers. When he later visited Corinth in Greece, we are told that Paul chose to lodge with two fellow tent-makers, Aquila and his wife Priscilla (*Acts* 18: 1-3). There are even hints, elsewhere in the New Testament, that Paul may have suffered from an eye affliction, perhaps caused by hours of weaving under poor light conditions (2 *Corinthians* 12: 7; *Galatians* 4: 13-15).

Both Tarsus and Laodiceia were situated on the important trade road that led from Antioch and the cities of the east through Asia Minor to Ephesus—a road that Paul used on his missionary journeys. Both cities had a large resident minority of Jewish traders and craftsmen. For example, in 59 BC the great Cicero defended Lucius Valerius Flaccus against charges of extortion, including one that involved more than twenty pounds of gold that had been raised by the Jews of Laodiceia to send to the Temple in Jerusalem (*pro Flacco* 68). Just as Tarsus was famous for its excellent woollen products, so too was Laodiceia—as was also the nearby city of Colossae, which had a small Christian community to whom Paul addressed one of his epistles.

What conclusions do I draw from this?

Firstly, I believe that what we have here is a plausible account of some at least of the factors that enabled the spread of a new, syncretic religion, along established trade routes and using commercial as well as personal contacts. Further evidence of the contacts between cities is provided by the *Homonoia* coins struck to celebrate city partnerships. Either as the active issuing mint or as the named "partner", Laodiceia appeared very frequently on these coins, the other cities including (at different periods) nearby Hierapolis, which was also important in the wool industry, Ephesus, which lay at the end of the great trade road from Antioch, and other major coastal cities like Smyrna, Pergamum and Nicomedia.

Secondly, I would argue that little stories like this are a reminder of something that we all too easily forget—that the dynamic cultures of the world are by definition not *fixed*, not *static*, and certainly not *pure*. If such processes can even be observed in the slow-moving, almost media-free world of the ancients, they are immeasurably more likely to be shaping our fast-moving modern world.

Cultural identity is contingent, but not only on the accident of birth in one part of the world rather than in another, and on our acculturation, but contingent also on our contacts, and on choice. A young man from London named Steven Georgiou, the son of a Greek-Cypriot father and a Swedish mother, turned himself into the international pop star Cat Stevens, who turned himself into the Muslim educationalist Yusuf Islam. There is (at least *in the long-term*) nothing immovable or intrinsic about cultural identity (the reason for the parenthetic qualification will become clearer later on). It's not genetic, and a culture can change. Moreover, we owe our cultural identity in a sense to others, because we can only define ourselves in terms of what we are not. We point the finger of scorn at our neighbors, at aliens, at outsiders, at the notorious Other, and by a process of out-grouping we fix and define the in-group that we belong to. By the same logic our cultural identity is contextual, shifting in accordance with where we are and whom we are dealing with. The English, Scots, Irish and Welsh have been squabbling for centuries, but, as George Orwell pointed out, "somehow these differences fade away the moment that any two Britons are confronted by a European" (83).

Those things within our culture which are most precious, that seem most typical, may actually be alien imports. Let us take some examples from food and drink: the Englishman with his tea—from India; the Italian with his pizza and pasta—using tomatoes, originally from America (and the name itself is actually Aztec); the Moroccan sipping his famous green tea with mint—tea, again, which the British introduced into Morocco in the eighteenth century (Bayart 1996, 68).

Conversely, what we imagine to be exotic may well be home-grown. One of the most popular dishes in Britain today is chicken tikka masala, which most people fondly believe to be an authentic Indian curry (and this is often quoted as an example of how multicultural and tolerant Britain has become).

But chicken tikka masala—literally, "spicy pieces of chicken"—is not from India. It was probably invented in the Seventies by a restaurant owner in Glasgow, who added a tomato-based sauce to a dry Indian chicken dish in order to satisfy his British customers, who never felt happier than when slopping tomato ketchup over their food (*Chicken tikka masala*, website). Incidentally, Germany's favorite snack meal, the *currywurst*, or "curry sausage", has even less to do with India, having been invented in either Berlin or Hamburg in the late Forties (*Berliner Currywurst*, website).

Even our most treasured images may be of very peculiar origin. For example, the national symbol of Wales is the dragon, but where does it come from? I've been to Wales many times and I can assure you that there aren't any dragons there! The probable explanation is that, nearly two thousand years ago, in Roman British times, the tribesmen of South Wales developed a liking for an exotic beast that was being carried about as a standard by the Roman troops, and they decided to make it their own. There are several possible candidates here. The creature that the Welsh so took to may have been the badge of the Second Augusta legion, a mythical being called the capricorn, which was half goat and half fish. Alternatively, it could have been the cavalry standard known as the *draco*, a serpent banner that may originally have been a wind-sock to help bowmen judge wind strength and direction. Whichever of these it was, it seems to have turned itself into the Welsh dragon. A similar deconstruction can be applied to many other popular cultural symbols and icons.

So—how seriously should we take cultural identity? Does it really exist? One of the most emphatic attacks on the culturalist position is Jean-François Bayart's book *The Illusion of Cultural*

Identity (1996). For Bayart,

> there is no such thing as culture, only operational acts
> of identification. The identities we talk about so pomp-
> ously, as if they existed independently of those who
> express them, are made (and unmade) only through
> the mediation of such identificatory acts, in short, by
> their enunciation (92).

Bayart is particularly fierce on the subject of the Rwandan
genocide of 1994, in which hundreds of thousands of people
were murdered because they supposedly belonged to the wrong
ethnic group, although the actual difference between Tutsis
and Hutus is very difficult to pin down genetically, culturally
or linguistically. For instance, in the colonial period, simply
the number of cattle that you had may have determined how
your ethnic identity was officially defined. "The prevalent view
has been that the 1933-34 census identified Tutsi as separate
from Hutu on the basis of the ten-cow rule: whoever owned
ten or more cows was classified as a Tutsi", writes Mahmood
Mamdani (2001, 98—though he goes on to argue that, albeit
that there is a "kernel of truth" to this story, it isn't the whole
explanation).

  Bayart is right about cultural identity—but he is also wrong.
He is throwing the baby out with the bathwater. An unpreju-
diced analysis, even a gentle deconstruction, of our more rigid
cultural viewpoints is what we need, not a full-scale frontal
attack on them. It is not so much *who* you are or *what* you are
that matters, but who or what you and other people *think* you are,
and we do still need culture. We need culture for the following
reasons:

  (1) to give us filters through which to experience and give
order to our environment;
  (2) to give us the survival rules for existing in our particular
society;

(3) and to give us a feeling of who we are and where it is that we belong.

Because—wherever it is that they may happen to come from—patterns of behavior, values and beliefs *do* differ between cultures. Cultural identity is a choice, made by individuals and by groups, and, once the choice has been made, it makes no difference whether the emblems, traditions and beliefs of that culture are original, stolen or synthetic. If they are believed in and cherished, they are of life-giving importance, a central core of, yes, *identity*, which has to be protected. Just because there can be no going back to the crude essentialism of fixed "national character" doesn't mean that members of a culture don't have a particular view of it, don't see themselves as belonging to it, and don't treasure what they hold to be its qualities, achievements and beauties, in all of which they may take a share. To borrow words used by Shakespeare's Othello (in a different context, admittedly, but the Moor of Venice's words fit well here, too), it is the place:

> [...] where I have garner'd up my heart,
> Where either I must live, or bear no life,
> The fountain, from the which my current runs,
> Or else dries up [...] (*Othello*, IV, 2, ll. 58-61).

If we accept that, even in postmodern times, there is something called "culture" that people believe in and which shapes their behavior patterns and values, we are immediately faced with the problem of how then to interact with *other* cultures, a problem for which there is no easy solution. Culturalists, wearing their cultural relativist hats, will say, "Fine! Cultures are different. Then let us agree to differ. And when in Rome, do as the Romans do. It is not for us to dictate how other people should organise their lives. That's racist, chauvinistic, imperialistic, *etc.*" But in practice it's not fine at all, just letting other people get on with what they want to do. It's not something we automatically accept on the micro-level. Who would sleep easy after discovering that their neighbor was kidnapping people, abusing them, perhaps murdering them and burying their bodies in his backyard? (Something which unfortunately occurs all too often in individualistic Western cultures, with their emphasis on individual rights, privacy, and so on.)

Today we are all neighbors, though, and in the globalized world of Google Maps, news networks, Facebook and Twitter it is *not* acceptable to tolerate gross acts of abuse and cruelty simply because "it's their culture". Religion and culture may be called upon to justify why women should be allowed to die if there are only male doctors available to treat them, or why young girls should be denied education, stoned to death for committing adultery (or for having the misfortune to be the victim of rape), or have their thumb-tips cut off as a punishment for wearing nail-varnish (Mishra 2006, 366). In the view of the universalists, accepting such arguments is a moral cop-out, a betrayal of the victims, the oppressed and the powerless, women, children, slaves, ethnic and religious minorities, eccentrics and non-conformists, for which there can be no excuse.

What I'm therefore advocating is a kind of culturally tolerant universalism—an unfashionable position, perhaps, but one that is becoming less unfashionable. A way needs to be found to proclaim and defend universal, humanistic values while at the same time leaving space for separate and different cultural traditions. I am fully aware that it will require a squaring of the circle. It might actually be impossible (although we won't know till we try). It's perhaps the *second* biggest problem facing the human race today (after climate and the environment).

Let me return to where I started, the topic of syncreticism. If we can admit our bastard cultural origins, our mixed race, our lack of cultural purity, in other words: if we could stop taking ourselves so seriously, though without denying who we think we are and what we believe in, it would be much easier for us to get along with each other, making those adjustments and compromises that the world increasingly needs. By establishing a common core of agreed values based on practical kindness and good will, we would be able to explore the real treasure house of human potential, namely the synergistic possibilities inherent in our rich cultural and intellectual differences. This, I believe, is the process, the *dialog*, that the title of this conference refers to.

References

Bayart, Jean-François. *The Illusion of Cultural Identity* [*L'Illusion Identitaire,* 1996]. London: Hurst, 2005.

Chicken tikka masala. Website, <http://en.wikipedia.org/wiki/Chicken_tikka_masala>

Cicero, Marcus Tullius. "*Pro Flacco* (The Speech in Defence of Lucius Valerius Flaccus)". In: *Cicero, X (The Loeb Classical Library, 324).* Transl. C. Macdonald. Cambridge, MA / London: Harvard University Press / Heinemann, 1976, 411-557.

Berliner Currywurst im Web, Die. Website, <http://www.currywurst-berlin.com/>

Dio Chrysostom. "The Thirty-Fourth, or Second Tarsic, Discourse." In: *Dio Chrysostom, III (The Loeb Classical Library, 358).* Transl. J. W. Cohoon / H. Lamar Crosby. Cambridge, MA / London: Harvard University Press / Heinemann, 1940, 335-87.

Jarman, Francis. "The Local Coinages of the Roman Empire as an Example of Syncretization and Cultural Survival in a Time of Globalization". In: *The Journal of Languages and Translation,* II, 3, 2, April 2006, 373-85.

Mamdani, Mahmood. *When Victims Become Killers: Colonialism, Nativism, and the Genocide in Rwanda* (2001). Paperback edition. Princeton, NJ: Princeton University Press, 2002.

Mishra, Pankaj. *Temptations of the West: How to Be Modern in India and Beyond* (2006). London: Picador, 2007.

Orwell, George [Eric Blair]. "The Lion and the Unicorn: Socialism and the English Genius, Part I: England Your England" (1941). In: *The Collected Essays, Journalism and*

Letters of George Orwell, II: My Country Right or Left, 1940-1943. Ed. Sonia Orwell / Ian Angus. Harmondsworth, Middx.: Penguin, 1970, 74-99.

Philostratus. *The Life of Apollonius of Tyana*, I *(The Loeb Classical Library, 16).* Transl. F. C. Conybeare. Cambridge, MA: Harvard University Press, 1912.

Shakespeare, William. *Othello.* Ed. M. R. Ridley. The Arden Edition of the Works of William Shakespeare. London / Cambridge, MA: Methuen / Harvard University Press, 1962.

ABOUT THE AUTHORS

Ghada M. Abdel Hafeez is a professor of English literature and head of the English Department at Minia University (Egypt). She's a Salzburg Seminar Fellow, having attended Session 408 on Contemporary American Literature: Cultural Diversity and Aesthetic Continuities (2003), as well as a senior consultant trainer for the ERP (Education Reform Program) and for the Ministry of Education.

Mirren Augustin teaches comparative cultural studies and intercultural communication at the University of Hildesheim. Born and bred in Germany, her origins lie in Scotland and her heart reaches out to Montreal in Canada, where she spent a happy year studying and immersing herself in French-speaking theater.

Anna Brünig studied international information management, psychology and political science at the University of Hildesheim. She is a convinced Italophile and whenever possible likes to spend time in her ancient farmhouse in the beautiful Apennine Mountains. Even after long years of research, some aspects of Italian life (such as certain politicians) are still a mystery to her.

María Elena Camacho-Mohr teaches Spanish and comparative cultural studies, with a focus on Latin America, and intercultural communication at the University of Hildesheim. She has lived a third of her life in Germany, but her roots are firmly planted in Mexico and Guatemala. Consistent with her multi-cultural background and interests, she has long been a student of the Mayan and Aztec civilizations, both ancient and modern.

Jürgen Einhoff was a teacher trainer for teachers of English before retiring in 2000, and then taught comparative cultural studies, focusing on the USA, at the University of Hildesheim for several years. He is an ardent advocate of systems theory and has published a number of articles and readers on language-teaching matters. His contribution to this volume reflects his own personal views and experiences. His London-born wife has—of course—been his greatest asset.

T. W. Geraghty has nothing to add to the information given in the interview, although it is known that he prefers the Irish sort of whiskey to any other kind.

Francis Jarman teaches comparative cultural studies and intercultural communication at the University of Hildesheim. According to family tradition, he is descended from the Thracian slave Androcles (of "Androcles and the Lion" fame). In 2009, Dr. Jarman was awarded the Erasmus Prize of the German Academic Exchange Service. He is also a playwright, novelist and classical numismatist.

Beatrix Kress studied Slavic and German language and litera-ture and is a professor of intercultural communication at the University of Hildesheim. As a student, she spent a happy semester in Prague and has tried to visit the Czech Republic as often as possible ever since. Besides Czech culture, she is also very interested in Russian language and literature.

Taina Niederwipper studied international information management, political science and history at the University of Hildesheim, where she is currently pursuing her doctorate, on Cypriot identities, in the Department of History. She tries to indulge in Cypriot realities on both sides of the island as often as possible, in order to understand the conflict from the inside. Other than that, Taina is fascinated by the whole business of film synchronization. May 4th is her favorite day of the year.

Premila Paul teaches literatures in English at the American College, Madurai, India. She has published on Indian literature and gender issues. She is actively involved in the development of the Study Center for Indian Literature in English and Translation (SCILET). Dr. Paul is full of *prem* (love) and SCILET is a labor of love for her.

Samah Tawhid Ahmed studied English language and literature at Cairo University in Beni-Suef, where she now teaches classes in English and is working to complete a thesis on John Okada and Monica Sone. Her favorite quote is the following from the Koran: "And of His signs is the creation of the heavens and the earth, and the difference of your languages and colors. Lo! herein indeed are portents for men of knowledge" (*ar-Rum* 22).

Claus Telge is enrolled in a joint PhD program (transcultural German studies / German as a foreign language) of the universities of Arizona and Leipzig, and is writing a dissertation on translations of South American and Spanish poetry into German by Erich Arendt and Hans Magnus Enzensberger. He is also lead singer and guitarist in the band The Cicada Piece.

Christoph Werner taught technical English and worked in English teacher training at various universities in East and West Germany before he retired to live in Weimar. He has published short stories and three novels, the most recent being *Buckingham Palace* (Bertuch, 2008). The Silberschlag crater on the moon is named after Dr. Werner's ancestor Johann Esaias Silberschlag (1721-91).